CONCILIUM

Religion in the Eighties

CONCILIUM

Concilium 199 (5/1988): Third World Theology

CONCILIUM

List of Members

Advisory Committee: Theology of the Third World

CONVERGENCES AND DIFFERENCES

Edited by
Leonardo Boff
and
Virgil Elizondo

English Language Editor
James Aitken Gardiner

T. & T. CLARK LTD
Edinburgh

August 1988
ISBN: 0 567 30079 X

ISSN: 0010-5236

Typeset by C. R. Barber & Partners (Highlands) Ltd, Fort William
Printed by Page Brothers (Norwich) Ltd

Concilium: Published February, April, June, August, October, December.
Subscriptions 1988: UK: £27.50 (including postage and packing); USA: US$49.95 (including air mail postage and packing); Canada: Canadian$59.95 (including air mail postage and packing); other countries: £27.50 (including postage and packing).

CONTENTS

CONVERGENCES
AND DIFFERENCES

Part IV
Evolution of Third World Theological Dialogue

Conclusion

CONVERGENCES AND DIFFERENCES

Editorial

IT SEEMS to be that nowhere in the Christian world has the teaching of Vatican Council II been taken more seriously and put into practice with greater vigour and creativity than in the Third World and among the oppressed minorities of the world. What we had been sensing in our innermost gut had to be done, we were now told to do by the Church! Out of this fidelity to the teachings of the Church, fascinating new aspects of church life are emerging out of the experience of the poor and the suffering, the marginalised and the unnoticed of the world.

Vatican II marked the greatest revolution in the Church since Constantine. Pastors from throughout the world gathered to reflect upon the meaning of revelation, Church, mission, worship, the Church in today's world and other related topics. The Church found itself to be a pilgrim group amongst other religious pilgrim groups. It recognised that the church itself in gradually growing into the fullness of truth (*Lumen Gentium* 4) and that this growth is *slow* and *strenuous* (*LG* 5). In this process of growth, it is helped by the other great religions of the world for they too are endowed with truth and holiness (*Nostra Aetate* 2). We as Catholics cannot stand isolated and apart from the other great religious traditions as if we alone had an exclusivity on divine truth. 'The Church therefore has this exhortation for her sons: prudently and lovingly, through dialogue and collaboration with the followers of other religions, and in witness of Christian faith and life, acknowledge, preserve and promote the spiritual and moral goods found among these persons, as well as the values in their society and culture.' (*NE* 2)

Nowhere in the world is this dialogue envisioned by the Council taking place is such a prolific way as in Asia where the Christians are truly a minority amongst peoples of other religions. The basic human communities made up of persons of various religions and of various ideological orientations all seeking together the common religious experience that comes when we truly seek to serve those in need, is providing a refreshing new breakthrough in the possibilities of fellowship. Out of these communal experiences, new understanding is emerging both about our own Christianity and about the other great religions. Tissa Balasuriya brings this out in a strikingly provocative article on the emerging theologies of Asia while Hyun-kyung Chung illustrates this with a specific article on Women-centred religion in Korea.

There has never been any question that the Church's basic constitution calls it to evangelise all peoples of the world. Yet what does it mean to evangelise? What does it mean to take the good news to the poor? Will the missionary preaching and conversions lead to truly new life or will it lead to the destruction of the people and their ways? The Church had a sad memory, especially since 1492, of allowing the saving word of God to go alongside with the destructive powers of the colonising nations which for centuries have dominated our Third World of today. For the peoples of the Third World—who really had no choice in receiving and accepting the missioners from the colonial powers—becoming Church often meant the fatal end of their customs, traditions, values and religious expression. The result has been that the Church has not been experienced as the sacrament of salvation but as the ultimate instrument of domination, for it appeared to justify the culture and customs of the oppressive colonisers. No matter how good or saintly the missionaries might have been, they were of the same human group and religion as those who oppressed and exploited the people!

Evangelisation as ethnocide could no longer continue. Vatican II in its decree on missionary activity returned to the earliest Christian tradition of evangelisation. It spoke about its mission to evangelise without destroying the native cultures, thus giving birth to truly local churches. The notion of a 'colonial church' would be a very contradiction of the churches which come forth according to the way of the Incarnation. The word of God is implanted in the local soil and from this a new local church is born. The young churches received 'from the customs and traditions of their people, from their wisdom and their learning, from their arts and their sciences' (*Ad Gentes* 22). For the young church to really take root and grow in strength and maturity 'theological investigation must necessarily be stirred up in each major socio-cultural area . . . in this way a fresh scrutiny will be brought to bear on the deeds and words which God has made known, which have been consigned to sacred Scripture, and which have been unfolded by the Church Father and the teaching authority of the Church ... Thus it will more clearly seen in what ways faith can seek for understanding in the philosophy and wisdom of these peoples' (*AG* 22).

Africa has certainly taken the lead in this type of socio-cultural dialogue between the Christian tradition as it has come to us through the centuries and the word of God as it had been present in the local customs, traditions and religions. The task of decolonising Christianity and allowing it to be truly incarnated has been the challenging work of the churches of Africa as presented by Engelbert Mveng. Yet, as Professor Mveng clearly points out, it is just a route. It is a project which unfolds day by day; and each day, new insights come forth which are relevant not just for Africa but for the universal Church.

But the Church at Vatican II went even further than religions and cultures. It had to be concerned, as the founder was, with the deepest concern denominator of the present day misery of the human situation: *poverty*. The Church already had a developing tradition of social teaching: of the need of the Church to be actively involved in working for change in the social order. Christians cannot remain indifferent to the cries of the poor. Social justice, proclaimed the Roman Synod, is an essentially ingredient of evangelisation. In the Constitution on the Church, it states: 'The Church encompasses with love all those who are afflicted with human weaknesses. . . . She does all she can to relieve their need and in them she strives to service Christ.' (*Lumen Gentium* 8). John XXIII, Paul VI and now John Paul II have been exhorting the world in an increasing powerful way about the need to create totally new civilisations. John Paul II has stated that the present civilisations are simply not capable of responding to the needs and miseries of the peoples of today. Bold and radical change is needed if humanity is to survive.

Latin America has certainly taken this exhortation seriously. Bishops, pastors, pastoral workers, theologians and lay people have begun to recommit themselves *to the poor* and to working *with the poor* for a *new humanity*. Millions across the Latin American continent are seeking for the God of life amid their death-bearing existence. Out of the deep and disastrous socio-economic oppressions, people are seeking new forms of life. It is out of Latin America that the universal Church hears the profoundly moving songs of praise of the poor. As Gustavo Gutierez brings out: 'How to sing the praises of God from among the sufferings of the innocent!'

No theological movement has ever challenged society and the churches as strongly and as rapidly as that which is emerging out of the millions of base community theologians of Latin America. We know some of the great names, but it is the entire ensemble of peoples who is truly doing this new theologising as Julio de Santa Ana, Leonardo Boff and Pablo Richard bring out. Out of the sufferings of the poor, the good news is irrupting.

Finally, the Church in Vatican II saw itself on the move 'like a pilgrim in a foreign land, presses forward amid the persecutions of the world and consolations of God'. (*LG* 8). No other human group can appreciate this reality more than the poor and oppressed minorities of the world who are always made to feel like foreigners who are at best tolerated. Yet out of this experience of being like pilgrims in a foreign land, refreshing new aspects about the innermost identity and mission of the Church come forth. An example of this has been the struggles of the minorities of the United States: the Blacks who were imported as slaves, the Hispanics who were conquered and forced to live as foreigners in their own land and the Native Americans who were put into concentration camps called 'Indian Reservations' and systematically denied a life of their own. Yet out of this dehumanising existence, new life is beginning to burst forth and new insight about the very innermost nature of Christianity itself: *a pilgrim in a foreign land*. James Cone brings this out as he explores the highlights of the minorities of the US.

Today, no individual or individual church can speak of the word of God by itself alone. To be credible, we must each seek to reflect seriously from our own situation, but remain in patient dialogue with others who are equally searching. John Paul II inaugurated a new era of this common search at Assisi where he prayed as an equal with other great religious leaders and the theologians of the Third World are equally inaugurating a new era in huamnity's quest for God and the ways of God. As Professor Mveng brings out: it is a route whose direction unfolds each day. But we are on the way. And the amazing thing is that from amongst those who often die way before their time because of malnutrition, disease and violence, the God of life is issuing a call to the entire planet to convert lest the entire planet cease to exist. *Out of those who are suffering death, the loudest cry for life is coming forth.*

In closing our introduction, it is important to note that the most fascinating and far-reaching aspects of the theologies which are arising out of the Third World are not to be found in the pages of published works but in the hand-written notes of the millions of ordinary people who are theologising out of their own living experiences of faith. It is here that the greatest breakthroughs are taking place. These theological works will not be studied by scholars or be quoted in other works, but they are truly doing what all theology should do: *animate, strengthen, correct* and *nourish* the life of the faithful.

Virgil Elizondo
Leonardo Boff

PART I

'Can Any Good Thing Come Out of Nazareth?'

Leonardo Boff

What are Third World Theologies?

TO UNDERSTAND what we mean by Third World theologies, we need first to clarify what we mean by the Third World. The expression 'Third World' was coined by the French sociologists in the fifties. It designates those countries that exist on the periphery of the industrialised capitalist world (the USA and Canada, Western Europe, Japan, Australasia, making up the 'First World') and outside the orbit of the socialist countries of Eastern Europe, including the USSR, which make up the 'Second World'.[1]

1. UNDERDEVELOPMENT, THE REVERSE OF THE DEVELOPMENT COIN

The main feature of the Third World is its underdevelopment.[2] The indices by which underdevelopment can be measured (and it will always be relative to what we understand by development and the indices which measure that) include:

(1) On the economic level, technological backwardness, the constant worsening of terms of trade between industrial goods (imported from the countries of the centre) and raw materials (exported by the countries of the periphery), and a high level of external debt;

(2) On the social level, widespread poverty on the one hand and great wealth of élites on the other, high figures of infant mortality, the marginalisation of the great mass of the population;

(3) On the political level, the weakness of institutions, the existence of

authoritarian governments, often highly repressive in character, the over-
riding of human and social rights;

(4) On the cultural level, illiteracy and the lack of participation by the
people in the processes of society; and finally,

(5) On the religious level, the churches' dependence on those of the centre
for resources of personnel and funds, and the proliferation of charismatic
sects, in which those who feel forsaken take refuge.

Practically all the nations of the Third World have one common
denominator: they were countries colonised by the European powers. For all
of them, colonisation was a complex and extremely traumatic process: it
brought domination in the military, economic, social, political, cultural and
religious spheres, and destroyed their indigenous cultures; it produced genocide in the countries of Central America and Mexico; it effected massive
deportation from one continent to another, as in the case of the blacks
shipped from Africa to North and South America and the Caribbean as
slaves. The political independence won by the countries of Latin America in
the nineteenth century and those of Africa in the twentieth did not have the
effect of liberating them from colonial rule, since external exploitation continued through the economic neo-colonialism of the industrialised nations,
coupled with internal exploitation by the oligarchies and bourgeoisie
associated with the interests of multinational capital. Alongside this type of
historical and social oppression, racial and sexual oppression also still
persist. Blacks, indigenous peoples, other ethnic minorities and women are
still continually discriminated against.[3]

It is not sufficient to describe the indices of poverty; it is more important
to identify the causes or conjuncture of factors that conspire to go on producing and reproducing it. Various models of understanding have emerged
over the past thirty years, which can be divided into the following stages:

(1) In the fifties, the poverty and backwardness of the Third World was
seen as a technical problem. All development required a series of steps, by
which a traditional society progressed into a modern society. The social
therapy for poverty was therefore to accelerate these steps through a gigantic
process of modernising industry, agriculture and the State. People then
talked of 'developing' countries. The churches took part in this process
through multiplying charitable organisations working to help the poor, opening schools in which new methods of agriculture, health care and work were
taught along with the faith. Pari passu, a theology of earthly realities, of
work of the world, emerged as the theological underpinning of the churches'
modernising activities.

This interpretation of steps to development and modernisation did not
produce satisfactory results. The route taken over the past two hundred

years by Europe and the United States simply cannot be reproduced today. Present conditions are completely different, since there were previously no dependencies such as those now, no monopoly of great capital enterprises nor the degree of competition that exists in the world market.

(2) These factors led, in the sixties, to another model for understanding the poverty of the Third World. More than a technical problem, it was a political problem. We all have to live in the same economic sphere (whether capitalist or socialist), but this sphere is not harmonious, since it includes rich nations, grouped round the North Atlantic, and poor nations, in the Southern hemisphere. The poverty of the Third World encourages the spread of Marxist revolutionary ideas and foments movements aiming at social change. So Marxism has to be forestalled by means of strengthening the links of interdependence through massive investment by the rich nations in the poor nations. So the various aid schemes came into being. People then spoke of developed and 'underdeveloped' countries within the same capitalist system. The social therapy for overcoming the miserable situation of the Third World was sought in deep changes in the habits of its population, in the means of production and in social relationships. The churches also took this reading of the situation on board and strongly supported reformist movements in various Third World countries. Theologies of development and progress appeared as a reflex response to this strategy.

All this vast effort, instead of narrowing the gap between rich and poor, increased it. In order to safeguard capitalist profits, military dictatorships were set up in most Third World countries, and an ideology of national security was instigated—the ideology of defence of capital, properly understood.[5] Reformism benefits the more advanced strata of society, penalises the marginalised, and leaves the socio-economic framework intact—and its logic will always be to produce more profit for the few and greater poverty for the many. Relations of interdependence can obtain only between advanced nations: between the advanced and the backward they can be of dependence only.

(3) Understanding of this fact led to the formulation of a third interpretation of underdevelopment in the seventies. It was seen as the reverse side of the coin of development in the capitalist mould. It is true that we are all involved in one process of development. But this process is profoundly unequal. The benefits of development are appropriated by the advanced strata of the Third World, while its counter effects are spread over the already disadvantaged sectors of the impoverished nations. The capitalism that exists in the poor countries is dependent on the capitalism of the centre, bound up with the interests of capital from the centre, and excludes the

great majorities of the people; it thereby produces a development of underdevelopment. In other words, the rich of the First World and the rich of the Third becomes continually *richer* at the expense of the poor who become steadily poorer. The well-being of the advanced societies of the First World is based on a massive exploitation, through multinational corporations, the inequality of terms of trade, the high cost of technology, the burden of foreign debt, of the countries of the Third World. These countries not merely *are* underdeveloped; they are coercively *held* in a state of underdevelopment within a framework of economic, political, cultural and even religious dependence.

This dependence is experienced as *oppression*, since these countries are prevented from developing a self-sustained historical-social project through being always dependent on and harnessed to the interests of the countries of the centre. If this dependence is oppression, then its reverse is liberation. It was in this sense that, in the early seventies, on the strictly analytical level, liberation began to be discussed as a correlative category opposed to oppression.[6]

2. THE IRRUPTION OF THE OPPRESSED INTO SOCIETY

Liberation theology cannot be understood without this socio-analytical reflection which has been undertaken throughout the Third World. But this reflection in turn supposes another, even more basic fact: the mobilisation of oppressed social groupings, or, in an expression dear to Latin American theology, the irruption of the poor on the scenario of society.[7]

Since the end of the second World War, capitalism, in its transnational form, has deeply penetrated the whole Third World. Its spread was favoured by the abundance of raw materials, the low cost of labour and State incentives. This penetration produced economies oriented to exports, a new transnationalised bourgeoisie, a new professional class tied to the interests of the world-wide system and a work force conscious of the power of capital over labour. This in turn produced a growing consciousness of the fact that the problems of the vast impoverished majorities could not be resolved by the methods of capitalist development. Something else was needed, on the lines of basic democracy of a popular stamp that would lead to a less conflictive society, allowing greater participation by all, starting with those marginalised by the ruling system.

So, throughout the Third World, trade unions with some political power appeared, as did parties linked to the interests of the workers, and popular associations of all kinds, in the country and cities. These were the oppressed

rising up like new barbarians, in the sense that they were those who were putting pressure on the 'empire', bearing a new social banner.[8] The response by the ruling system was an effort to co-opt these masses who were claiming their rights and demanding a structural change in society. 'Populism' was a politics practised by the ruling classes through charismatic leaders who listened to the people's demands without actually risking the basic interests of the ruling classes, who still kept their social hegemony. When populism failed to stem the people's desire for change, the liberal-bourgeois State turned to political repression, to the point of State terrorism in some cases. This terrorism, with its resultant systematic violation of all rights, was applied above all where guerilla and other insurrectionist movements appeared, particularly in Africa and Latin America.

Many Christians also took part in the movements of opposition to the ruling order, seen by the majority as the order of disorder. Their analytical discourse was of dependence-liberation and their political ideal based on democratic and socialist ideas. They were either those poor Christians most conscious of the contradictions of the capitalist system or Christians from other social classes who had made an option for the people and for transforming society in the interests of the majority. They asked themselves these questions: how can we be Christians in a world of destruction? How can the Christian faith become a factor in the liberation of the oppressed and everyone else, and stop being a bulwark of the unjust 'establishment'? These questions led to practical courses of action for Christians working with others who also sought liberation, and to corresponding thought stemming from these courses of action. Liberation theology is simply the most articulate and systematic response to these questions in the order of practice. But this response would not have been possible without the existence of favourable pre-conditions inside the churches, particularly the Catholic Churches.

3. THE CHURCHES' OPTION FOR THE POOR AGAINST THEIR POVERTY

In the peripheral, ex-colonial countries, the churches formed part of the structure that made for domination. Here and there the churches always contained pockets of those who supported the natives and blacks, but these were prophetic minorities; the churches as a whole, through their presence and activities, upheld the ruling order, which, seen from the viewpoint of the conquered and dominated, was that of invasion and violence. Nevertheless, in Africa starting with the independence and political liberation of several countries,[9] in Latin America from the 1950's and in Asia with the movement of inculturation of the Gospel in native cultures older than Western cultures,[10] and above all since Vatican II, the churches gradually broke their neo-colonial pact. Significant sectors began to support international, popular and liberating movements. In this, lay men and women committed to changing society played an important part. It was they who helped the government of the churches (the hierarchy) to understand Christianity's new historical-social mission in favour of oppressed, best expressed in the well-known phrase 'preferential option for the poor'.

This led to the development of a pastoral outlook more in tune with the needs of the people, more based in their midst and adapted to national cultures; bishops and priest appeared who were more pastors than ecclesiastical authorities, as did prophets who denounced social injustices and proclaimed the changes needed, and militant Christians in various Church and social movements dedicated to liberating action against the ruling order. The churches themselves, as was the case in Latin America, organised internally so that their activity could in itself be a form of liberation. So there emerged the thousands of base communities, in which the faithful experience their faith as bound up with the problems of poverty (so pointing up the liberating dimension of faith), reflect on their social responsibility, develop a critical consciousness of the structural causes of the poverty they suffer and decide on courses of action, as communities or as part of broader popular movements of secular origin. Besides these, there are also thousands upon thousands of Bible study groups in which commentary on the word of God has been taken over by the people themselves, producing a new view of faith, less abstract and dogmatic, more historical and tied to the ethical demands of justice and solidarity. The fact that many church people have taken part in popular movements, which are conflictive by their nature, has meant that many have been persecuted, arrested, tortured and even killed by the security and repressive forces of the ruling system. Almost all the churches of the Third World have produced martyrs as a result of their evangelical commitment to the poor and justice for them.

It was on the basis of this reality, composed of actions designed to change the historical course of society, that the type of reflection known as liberation theology emerged. On the Catholic side, this presupposed Vatican II's opening out to the modern world, to secular culture, science and technology and the questions involved in development. Applying this opening-out in the specific conditions of the Third World showed that science and technology were not only instruments through which human beings took control of nature, but that they also provided the main instruments of domination by the advanced countries over the scientifically and technically backward ones; it also showed that development is paid for by underdevelopment in the countries situated on the periphery of the capitalist empire; it showed too that there is not just 'the world', but a veritable sub-world of destitution and social injustice. The reception of Vatican II in the Third World made the rise of liberation theology in Catholic circles possible.[11] The fundamental question ceased to be the relationship between science and faith, or between mankind come of age and secularised and the Church, but that between faith and social injustice, between the Gospel and sub-humanity and sub-development. Hunger for bread linked to hunger for God gave rise to the concept of liberation as the way, through the power of faith, to achieve the social transformation that will guarantee that all have bread. In Latin America it was, therefore, the perception of economic-social destitutuion as a product of development in the capitalist mould that created the conditions that gave rise to liberation theology.

In Africa, destitution is probably even worse than in Latin America. But historical and social conditioning is different. Here the need to preserve native cultures invaded and subjected by European colonisation and the virulence of modern science and technology led Christians to work out a theology of liberation that would build on the cultural roots of the people while lifting them out of the anthropological poverty in which they were submerged. In Asia the main challenge comes from the religions, which are generally little concerned with the need for social change, while possessing aspects and intuitions that can be developed in the direction of specific liberation; this is the way in which fruitful dialogue and collaboration are opening up between them and a Christianity which is taking on its liberating function in society in the face of massive poverty and because of its own religious experience.

4. LIBERATION THEOLOGY: THE THEORY OF LIBERATION PRACTICE

Before discussing liberation theology as a theology typical of the Third World, it is as well to remember that there are also theologies in the Third World. There is a neo-scholastic theology similar to that produced in the First World, whose main concern is to explain and develop the official teaching of the Church. There is also a modern, progressive theology, the echo and counterpart of the main theological currents of the First World, which debates the questions of the modern age and issues of justice and peace. These are theologies in the Third World, but cannot be called theologies of the Third World, because they do not make the problems of the Third World the central axis of their discourse.

Liberation theology in Asia, Africa and Latin America sets out to examine the faith from the wretched situation in which the Third World finds itself.

Specifically, it arose in groups that met, and meet, in liberating practice aimed not at reform or aid, but at providing an alternative social system to the present one. It is not a matter of reflecting on the *subject* of oppression/liberation (as might be done in the corresponding entry in a theological or biblical dictionary); such reflection has always been part of theology, and the subject itself cannot force theology to change its method. The novelty liberation theology claims consists in its being a reflection in faith worked out from within a *practice* of liberation carried out by the oppressed in their movements. The first word is spoken by what is done, that is, by a conscious act aimed at changing social relationships. It is therefore an inductive theology. It does not start with words (those of the Bible or the magisterium) and end in words (new theological formulations), but stems from actions and struggles and works out a theoretical structure to throw light on and examine these actions.

The 'practice' of which liberation theology is the theoretical expression operates on various levels. It can be *pastoral* practice: how far catecheses, the liturgy and specifically religious acts awaken people to a consciousness of social sin and mobilise them to a commitment to change in the direction of justice. It can be *ecclesial-political* practice: to what extent Christians (the Church as a whole or parts of it) should join in movements to change society and seek an alternative that offers greater life and liberty to the oppressed and everyone else. Finally, it can be strictly *political* practice: those actions that bear directly on the transformation of society starting from the interests of its marginalised sectors. Such practice, though secular, still has an objective theological dimension, in so far as it can generate greater justice and dignity for all citizens, qualities that faith sees as belonging to the good things of the Kingdom of God. The Kingdom of God is much more than these, but it would not be the Kingdom without them. So liberation theology is critical reflection on human practice (of human beings in general and Christians in particular) in the light of Jesus' practice and the demands of the Gospel, carried out in order to improve this practice and make it more effective.

Social Analysis and Theology

Liberation theology is concerned with efficacy, since its purpose is to help in the actual liberation of the oppressed. But good intentions are not enough: it is also necessary to analyse the mechanisms that generate impoverishment, and to understand the pedagogical, political and religious ways to liberation. Without a thorough analysis of society it is easy to fall into the pitfalls mentioned above: reliance on aid, thereby helping the poor without challenging the rich, or reformism, which attacks the harmful effects of the system without discerning the roots that hold the society for which an alternative is sought in place. Liberation supposes the possibility of moving beyond this sort of development which costs the huge poor majorities so dear. What tools should it use for its analysis? No analyst works in a vacuum: the choice of a particular sort of analysis—functional or structural-dialectical, let us say, to choose the main types—refers back to the social context (the totality of interests involved, whatever project of society is aimed at) of the analyst. Those who come from a social system from which they benefit, tend to use arguments that justify and seek to improve this system. Those who suffer from the system under which they live tend to use arguments designed to change and indeed replace it.

Liberation theology makes a preferential and evangelical option for the oppressed; it tries to look at society from the standpoint of what will help in their liberation, and through their eyes. The structural-dialectical type of analysis suits this option better. There is nothing fortuitous in the fact that many Third World theologians use some basic concepts from Marxism in their analyses, since these help the poor to discover that they are not simply poor but also exploited and oppressed. Note that these theologians are not using Marxism in order to reach the people; they are using their experience of a poor Christian people to reach Marxism.[12] Their use of certain Marxist categories is purely instrumental, in the service of denouncing the mechanisms that generate poverty.

Just analysing society is not enough. It is also necessary to have a pedagogy for raising the consciousness of and liberating the oppressed. One of the basic concerns of liberation theology has been to develop a practical pedagogy of the oppressed and of education as practice of freedom, redeemed from the slavery of oppression.

Who are the agents of liberation, those who carry it out? Not the ruling classes, since they would have to fight against themselves, since they are a major (though not the only) cause of oppression. Not the State, since it, generally speaking, acts as an instrument for safeguarding the interests of those who hold power, knowledge and possessions, the groups that produce and reproduce the mechanisms of oppression and marginalisation, even though the State can contain opposing forces that benefit the humbler classes. Not the churches either, since they operate in the symbolic sphere of producing rationales and messages—important, but in themselves incapable of bringing about the liberation of the oppressed. Those who bring about liberation are the impoverished themselves, with their allies, becoming conscious of their oppression, organising themselves, projecting their vision of society and struggling for their freedom—which will in the end benefit everyone and not just themselves. If the oppressed do not take up the cause of their own liberation, this will not come from anywhere. This is the basic conviction of liberation theology.

Once this analysis has been made, for the sake of making liberating practice effective, the task of theology is to make a theological judgement on the facts that have come to light, so as to put forward specific courses of action that will start the process of liberation moving. These are the now familiar methodological steps of liberation theology: *seeing* ananlytically, *judging* theologically and *acting* pastorally or politically, three phases in one commitment in faith.

5. WHAT CONTRIBUTION HAS LIBERATION THEOLOGY MADE TO THEOLOGY IN GENERAL?

In the first place, liberation theology can claim the merit of having set the poor, their suffering and their cause, at the forefront of its thinking. It is from the standpoint of the poor that Jesus' message is seen as good news. The viewpoint of the poor allows us to recover the image of God as God of life, of Jesus as liberator, of the Spirit as principle of freedom, of the Church as the People of God, and so on. Theology does not claim to take the place of the voice of the poor, but to strengthen it, since they are the agents of liberation.

Secondly, this theology has recaptured the revolutionary nature of Christianity. It has freed it from the slavery of capitalism, from being the power that upheld the order created by capitalism, which is profoundly unfavourable to the poor. It has also taken away the monopoly held by Marxism on the ideal of transforming society. In the name of the God of life and Jesus Christ liberator, whole churches are taking up a stance of protest against social oppressions, and of solidarity with liberation movements, thereby demonstrating the liberating dimension of faith.

Thirdly, this theology has been responsible for making the actual practice of the people—what they do and what affects them in the spheres of economics, politics, sociology and ideology—the object of theological reflection, rather then some abstract concern always outside the scope of an always conflictive history. It was worked out an original hermeneutic through which it articulates the discourse of faith with the discourse of society, from the viewpoint of the oppressed. In doing so it recognises that the social sciences are not a formal constituent of theology, and safeguard the 'theologicity' of theology by using them as a means to understanding society in order to make the faith efficacious in history, something that has always been the concern of theology.[13]

Fourthly, liberation theology has defined another place in which theology is 'done': not so much the university or institute and more the community and in service to the community. There is a deep sense of Church in liberation theology because it is done in conjunction with pastoral work and pastoral workers. Those who do this theology are not so much individual theologians as the communities who bring their problems, solutions, actions and thinking to be taken up and worked on by theologians. Liberation theology has also brought about the rise of a *people's theology*, made by pastoral workers and committed Christians.

Fifthly, liberation theology has redeemed the evangelising character that all Christian thinking should have. It should bring people the good news of liberation and hope. To do this, it is not enough for theology to be orthodox; it must also take the risk of thinking out the vital and dramatic questions affecting the lives of persons and societies, offering them comfort and the promise of salvation.

Finally, liberation theology is a persecuted theology. The ruling classes accuse it of being Marxist and of fomenting the class struggle. But this is a pretext for avoiding any change and turning aside the political questions posed to them by the presence of the poor. Within the churches, there are those who accuse it of politicising the faith and creating a parallel church. Whilst I accept that there have been some excesses, this is generally a way of not taking the preferential option for the poor seriously, and of failing to meet the challenge of the base Church communities, which are forcing them to rethink the social division of religious work and give a more prominent place to lay people, women especially, in the churches. Theologians need to see this situation as one form of living the spirit of 'blessed are you when men persecute you' and of sharing the far more lacerating sufferings of the oppressed people.

Liberation theology, for the first time in church history, making heard the articulated cry of the oppressed calling on the centre from the periphery. In various churches, the centre has heard their clamour. Now we need to watch that it is not assimilated in a spiritualistic and moralistic fashion and so incorporated into the fabric of existing institutions, but continues to be a leaven for transforming society into a more equitable and human form, from within which the churches will emerge more evangelical—poorer—in greater solidarity with the victims of society.

Translated by Paul Burns

Notes

1. See *Theology from the Third World*, the final documents of the first five international congresses of the Ecumenical Association of Third World Theologians (EATWOT) (San José, Costa Rica, 1982) pp. 12–18.

2. See P. Rigol *Sociologia do Terceiro Mundo* (Petrópolis, 1977) with bibliography.

3. I regard Black theology of liberation, ethnic minority theologies and those currents of feminist theology that consider questions of class as well as of sex as Third World theologies. They are worked out from situations similar to those of the Third World, in the geo-political sense. There is a First World in the Third World, just as there is a Third World in the First.

4. Still the basic guide is G. Gutiérrez *A Theology of Liberation* (Maryknoll, NY & London, 1973).

5. See J. Comblin *La Iglesia y la ideología de la Seguridad Nacional*(Lima 1977); *Bibliographie sur la Sécurité Nationale* (Paris 1976).

6. H. Assmann *Opresión-Liberaciòn: desafio a los Cristianos* (Montevideo 1971); J. Miguez Bonino *Doing Theology in a Revolutionary Situation* (Philadelphia 1975), pp.1–60.

7. G. Gutiérrez *The Power of the Poor in History*(Maryknoll New York 1984).

8. A good summary is T. Buhl 'La teología de la liberación. Aspectos fundamentales de sus posiciones socio-políticas' in *Asia, Africa, Latin America* 20 (Berlin 1988) 64–96.

9. See S. Torres & V. Fabella (eds) 'O evangelho emergente' (São Paulo 1982) with the main contributions from Africa on pp. 31–126; A. Mbembe *Afriques indociles* (paris 1988) pp. 152–77.

10. S. Arokiasmamy & G. Gispert-Sauch *Liberation in Asia* (Delhi 1987).

11. See L. Boff 'A teologia da libertação: recepção criativa do Vaticano II na ótica dos pobres' in *Do lugar dos pobres* (Petrópolis 1984) pp. 13–43.

12. See O. Madura 'Demistificación del marxismo en la trología de la liberación' in REB 47 (1988).

13. See the important work by C. Boff *Theology and Praxis: Epistemological Foundations* (Maryknoll, New York 1987).

PART II

'These Dry Bones Live'

Engelbert Mveng

African Liberation Theology

1. DEFINITION OF AFRICAN LIBERATION THEOLOGY

THE FOUNDERS of the *Association Oecuménique des Théologiens Africains* began their Accra Declaration with a profession of faith which said: 'We realise that African unity is the unity of spirit and soul, an individual unity in historical reality which can overcome the inability to communicate geographically. Our unity is that of active participation in the full community of God: it is not lost in the mists of a vague universalism. We have also realised that threats hang over the unity of our race and we regret all those factors which tend to shake the solidity of our deeply rooted unity, whether economic isolation, power struggles or even different life styles.'

The history of the African Theological Movement has demonstrated the internal unity of this movement. The Accra Congress merely confirmed and accepted this unity which is identified with the historical destiny of a race in search of its salvation. For this reason one can distinguish under the following characteristics the specific aspects of Black African theology.

It is a theology of the people. It expresses the faith and hope of our oppressed peoples. It illustrates the experience of the living Christian communities in Africa. It is therefore not an academic theology, even if some of its promoters move in university circles. All present African theologians are from the lower classes, sons of peasants, artisans, clerks or churchmen rooted in their territory or in the very flesh of their tribalism. They are also sons of that African church whose living stones they are, and which cannot increase and prosper without the strength of their blood, their sweat and their faith. When the objection is made that this theology is not written in native languages, we reply that it is *lived* in native languages, in the villages and the neighbourhoods, before being translated into foreign languages by its own rightful heirs, the African theologians.

African theology is, by definition, contextual and its proper context is all Africa that we all know today as our home. This Africa has a long history of slavery, colonisation, oppression and domination. Today it is stifling under neo-colonialism, droughts, famines, disease, political crises, coups d'état, totalitarian regimes, disregard for the rights of man ... etc. The context of African theology is the life of our states, our peoples, our churches, with the numerous challenges which they have to face: political, economic, cultural and religious. Theology is a spiritual mobilisation to help God's people to face these challenges.

African theology is a Theology of Inculturation. By African culture, we mean the vision of the world and the conception of man and God which constitute both the source of inspiration and the mainspring of the creative genius of people when this genius is expressed through art, religion, economics, social and political life, etc. When we speak of inculturation, we mean the evangelisation of African culture in such a way as to enable it to be integrated into the eternal Christian heritage and to continue to make this heritage more 'catholic'. And on the other hand we mean the Africanisation of Christianity to the point where it becomes a constituent of the spiritual and cultural inheritance of Africa. That is the task assigned to African Liberation Theology. This task demands of every African theologian a very great mastery of his own culture. It is one of the major demands of this stage in the history of the Church of Africa, known as the *Second Evangelisation*. Its outcome will be the transition from the conversion of individuals and groups to the conversion to Christianity of a whole race, its way of life and thought.

African Liberation Theology is ecumenical. It is certainly not a matter of that institutionalisation of the division of churches which passes for ecumenism in certain countries. It is rather that African force for unity, reconciliation and solidarity which is deeply rooted in the purest tradition of their ancestors. Africa must invent its path to ecumenism and progress to the liberation of churches enchained by centuries of rivalry, divisions and power struggles.

African theology is a struggle for spiritual liberation. It opens the way to a spirituality of liberation which is the spirituality of the Beatitudes of the Gospels. The message of the Beatitudes proclaims the establishment of the Kingdom of God on the ruins of the kingdom of this world. The kingdom of the world is defined by the law of injustice and death; it is expressed in terms of possession, domination, oppression ... etc. It is the kingdom of those who are full and who laugh now. (Luke 6) This kingdom breeds poverty, destitution, injustice, tears, hard-heartedness, iniquity, discord and war, intolerance and persecution. It is from this kingdom that we must free ourselves and our brothers, in order finally to establish the Kingdom of God from where poverty, injustice, oppression, domination and persecution are abolished. It is the kingdom of truth, freedom, justice and love. This is the kingdom which we must establish in us and around us. The spirituality of the Gospel Beatitudes which is the spirituality of liberation, is not the eschatological result of Liberation theology but its theological foundation. While integrating political, economic, social and cultural contingencies, it allows ideological recoveries and the opportunism of 'actuality' to be transcended, in order to take root in universality and history. Within and beyond the theology of Liberation is to be found the spirituality of Liberation. It opens the way to a meeting with the historical Christ without our struggles for freedom. The spirituality of the Beatitudes then concerns all men, those in the Third World as well as all the others, for everyone must choose between the servitude of the kingdom of this world and the freedom to be found in the joy of building the Kingdom of God. It is the spirituality of the Beatitudes which allows us to put our finger on the universal character of Liberation theology. Every sinner is a slave to be freed through Jesus Christ. For us Africans, if Liberation Theology was invented by the Third World, it is in reality the theology of all sincere Christians and therefore of the Universal Church.

2. EXTENSION OF AFRICAN LIBERATION THEOLOGY

African theology is on the move. It is more and more a project in the process of development which becomes reality as it spreads. It is not a hidden treasure, a deposit shut away in the secret coffers of an arrogant and stony dogmatism.

On the contrary, African theology appears as an awakening by African Christian communities of their experience of faith in Jesus Christ. This experience is not most important thing. The words which express it must as far as possible be the faithful reflection of this experience. African reality today is that of a fragmented and traumatised continent. Many of those interested in African theology present it in the light of this fragmentation. There are three main zones: anglophone Africa, francophone Africa and South Africa.[1] They represent in fact the regions in which theological activity is most intense.

(i) *Anglophone Africa* includes the greatest number of theological Institutions, not only because of the importance of the denominational foundations for the training of ministers in religion, but more because of the university system which integrates the Institutes of religious sciences into the State Universities. The great majority of the 450 establishments registered in Africa in 1984 and figuring in the *Directory of Theological Institutions in Africa* published by the *Lutheran World Federation*, belong to anglophone Africa. The same can be said of the 14 Associations with theological aims, and the 65 theological revues and periodicals mentioned in the same Directory. A separate place must be reserved for the *Bulletin de Théologie Africaine*, the organ of the *Association Oecuménique des Théologiens Africains*. Unfortunately, these Institutions are often a curb to the emergence of an authentically African theology. The contribution of anglophone Africa to African theology is less the work of the Theological Institutions that that of committed theologians. Their names and their works are well known. The following have become classic: J. Mbiti (Uganda), Nyamiti (Uganda), John Pobee, Kwesi Dickson (Ghana), Bolaji Idowu and Eugene Uzukwu (Nigeria), Zablon Nthamburi (Kenya), Laurenti Magesa (Tanzania), Justin S Ukpong (Nigeria), Harry Sawyer (Sierrra Leone), Sarpong (Ghana), Kalilombe (Malawi).[2]

Their works treat practically the same themes which are found in the theologians of francophone Africa: the Bible, African religions, inculturation, liberation, ecumenism, Christology, ecclesiology. The two cultural movements of contemporary Africa are usually presented as conflicting: *the African personality* for the anglophones, *negritude* for the francophones. Apart from the fact that these movements represent a byegone historical age, their opposition is only in form; the content is the same: the black man's struggle for liberation. So it cannot be said that there is a theology of anglophone Africa which is fundamentally different from that of francophone Africa. They are two facets of a single reality.

(ii) *Francophone Africa*

Although it has a more modest number of theological Institutions, francophone Africa has a much more abundant theological production. It is sufficient to consult the bibliography published by the *Bulletin de Théologie Africaine* (B.P. 823, Kinshasa XI, Zaire).

Apart from seminaries, both large and small, there are only two Faculties of Catholic Theology in francophone Africa, the Faculty at Abidjan (Ivory Coast) and at Kinshasa (Zaire). There are plans for a third Faculty at Yaoundé, in Cameroon. The Protestants, for their part, have a Theology Faculty at Kinshasa, at Bangui, at Yaoundé, at Tananarivi ... In all, six

Theology Faculties out of the forty Universities of theological teaching in the African continent.

Here, as in the anglophone zone, it is often not in the official theological Institutions that pioneers for an African Liberation theology are to be found.

However, it is important to emphasise that in francophone Africa the Negritude Movement first, then the *Association Oecuménique des Théologiens Africains*, have contributed substantially to the expansion of an authentically African theology. The Kinshasa Faculty of Catholic Theology, breaking with the conservatism of the other theological Institutions, has become an astonishingly fruitful centre of theological creativity whose dynamism is perhaps unique in Africa.

The *Bulletin de Théologie Africaine*, the organ of the *Association Oecuménique des Théologiens Africains*, has in turn become the best vehicle for African theological thinking in the world. So there are, on the whole, certain favourable conditions which facilitate the birth and diffusion of Liberation theology in francophone Africa and in the world.

All the foregoing explains why theological production is more abundant in francophone countries.

African theologians are perhaps more numerous there. Like their anglophone brothers, they are committed, militant, even controversial. What do they discuss in their works? Practically the same themes and the same problems as their anglophone brothers; but often from different approaches. Chronologically, the debate on Black African culture dominated the period 1945–1960, with the foundation of the *Société Africaine de Culture* (SAC.) and the review *Présence Africaine* (1947). The most famous names in this connection are Aimé Césaire and L. S. Senghor, the fathers of negritude; then Alioune Diop, general secretary of the SAC, and founder of Présence Africaine; Sheikh Anta Diop, the author of *Nation Nègre et Culture*;[3] Keita Fodeba, Director of the Guinea Ballet, who revealed to the world the rich splendours of Guinean music and choreography; Franz Fanon, author of *Peau Noire et Masques Blancs* (1952), and all the first generation of African novelists. Among the leaders of this cultural struggle, African churchmen took their place in the front line: Vincent Mulago, Alexis Kagame, Tharcisse Tshibangu, Robert Sastre, Meinrad Hebga[4] . . . It was at this time that I began publication of my articles on African Art, in the review *Abbia* in Yaoundé and in *Présence Africaine* (1958).

In a way, this period marks the peak of the cultural revolution triggered off by negritude.

The year 1956 was at the same time the year of Aimé Césaire's *Lettre à Maurice Thorez*, of Sheikh Anta Diop's (unaccepted) thesis on *Nation Nègre et Culture*, and of *Prêtres Noirs s'interrogent*. This last work is considered as the starting point of the modern African Theology Movement. In fact, it may be said that the debate began in 1948 with the publication, in *Présence Africaine* editions, of the work of the Belgian Franciscan missionary, the R. P. Placide Tempels, a work entitled *La Philosophie Bantoue*.[5] This work was followed in 1950 by Aimé Césaire's *Discours sur le Colonialisme*; in 1951 by the Rev. Pere Th. Theuws article on *Philosophie Bantoue et Philosophie Occidentale*;[6] in 1952 by Eugene Guernier's work on *L'Apport de l'Afrique Noire à la Pensée Humaine* (Paris 1952); in 1954 by Vincent Mulago's thesis on *L'Union Vitale Bantu . . . Face à l'Union Vitale Ecclésiale* (Rome); in 1955 by Alexis Kagame's *De la Philosophie Banturwandaise de l'Etre*.[7] In 1956 also took place the 1st Congress of black writers and artists, organised in Paris by *Présence Africaine*. It was at this time that a group of 11 black priests from Africa and the Diaspora, following a poll conducted by *Présence Africaine*, published *Des Prêtres Noirs s'interrogent*, a small 288 page work with a modest, even timid, title, which was soon to be welcomed as the first manifesto of modern Black African Theology.[8] The main subject of this work is well and truly the problem of Inculturation. This was nearly 10 years before the Second Vatican Council, 12 years before the Conference of Latin-American Bishops at Medellin (1968), 23 years before Puebla (1979).

The debate on African theology came into the public domain with *Des Prêtres Noirs s'interrogent*. The *Philosophie Bantoue* of Fr. Tempels had been greeted with scepticism, even with irony. The work of the black priests provoked a certain annoyance in some quarters. It can be said that the period 1956–1970 was the period of the great debate on African theology. The opponents were drawn from the missionaries and the professionals of Western theology. There were some people of stature among them, like Canon Vanneste, one of the founders of the Lovanium, Professor, then Dean, of what was to become the Faculty of Catholic Theology at Kinshasa. He was finally to surrender and be converted to African theology.[9] Others showed their anxiety or their scepticism; notably Grahay, Matthews, Murray and Poulton.[10] Faced with these, the African theologians raised the impregnable wall of their arguments, their faith and their ability. In the forefront were Tshibangu, Mulago, Kagame, Lufuluabo, Malula, Tchidimbo, Mebga, Sanon, followed by Father Mveng, Ngindu Mushete, Eboussi-Boulaga, Mudinbe, Ntabona . . . and a group of other young philosophers and theologians, some of whom were to become enmeshed in the hair-splitting intricacies of the argument over the possibility of an African theology or way of thinking.[11] It was during this period that African theology became formally established. The African struggle for culture and brought off splendid victories. In 1959, the 2nd Congress of Black writers and artists was held in Rome. The two chosen themes were: *The Unity of Black African Cultures* and *The Responsibility of Men of Culture*. The participants were received in audience by Pope John XXIII. Other cultural and theological events mark the same period:

1961: Abidjan Symposium on Religions as Values of Civilisation. This symposium was organised by *Présence Africaine*.

1963: On the eve of the 2nd Vatican Council, *Présence Africaine* published *Personnalité Africaine et Catholicisme*. It was both a sequel to the publication of the Black Priests in 1956 and an African contribution to the preparation for the Council. Following this volume, the *Société Africaine de Culture* decided to launch a bulletin: *L'Afrique au Concile*. Unfortunately this bulletin only appeared once.

Meanwhile, in Africa itself, theological activity became more and more intense. Three theological weeks were organised at Kinshasa, then Léopold-ville, by the new Catholic University, the Lovanium, in 1954, 1965 and 1966. They were followed in 1968 by the *Symposium on African Theology* and in 1969 by a theological week on: *Renewal of the Church and New Churches*.

It should be noted here that 1966 was also the year of the first world Festival of Black Arts, organised in Dakar by President Léopold Sédar Senghor.

Even though in 1970 it can be said that African theology had become firmly established, it must also be recognised that until 1976–1977, African theologians, divided by colonial linguistic barriers, were to work incoherently, in scattered ranks. From 5 to 12 August 1976 the Constituent Assembly of the Ecumenical Association of Third World Theologians met at Dar-es-Salaam, in Tanzania. It was here that the African participants conceived the idea of creating an exclusively African association. The following year, at Accra in Ghana, on the occasion of the first meeting of the Ecumenical Association of Third World Theologians, the African participants created the *Association Oecuménique des Théologiens Africains*. Following the Accra Declaration, African theologians from now on would work on a united front, francophones, anglophones, lusophones, arabophones, as well as our black brothers in South Africa, within our *Association Oecuménique des Théologiens Africains*.

(iii) *South Africa*

It is perhaps the moment to discuss the question of Black theology in South Africa. In the first part of this paper, we have seen the emergence of this theology over a century and a half, through the dramatic experience of the Independent Churches. The protests of Blacks despised, oppressed, enslaved, have long been confined to the ghetto of sects and tribal churches. The new fact in South Africa is that these protests are henceforth taken up by the official churches: the Liberation theology of the Blacks in South Africa is now considered as one of the peaks of Christian experience in its universality.

Black African theology, in its heroic struggle for the dignity and cultural identity of the black man, just as much as North American Black theology, has certainly played a considerable role in this development. More than once, before 1976, Desmond Tutu and Alan Boesak had appeared at African Christian conferences. They represented in our eyes the suffering humanity of South Africa. They also represented the churches which were victims of the divisions and contradictions of South African racism. The shock caused by the emergence of 'Black Power' in the United States helped to bring our brothers out of their isolation. But, from the establishment of the Ecumenical Association of Third World Theologians at Dar-es-Salaam in 1976 we issued an urgent appeal to our South African brothers to bind our solidarity once and for all. They were at our side, in Accra, on that night of 20 December 1977 when we created the *Association Oecuménique des Théologiens Africains*. Their representatives were Alan Boesak and Gabriel M. Setiloane; for us they represent the whole of the Black people and all the churches in South Africa. Others—younger and more numerous—have since joined the ranks of the A. O. T. A.: Bongajalo Goba, Simon Maimela and Franck Chikane . . .

All these friends from the two associations of African theologians and of Third World theologians are today in the front line of the struggle for freedom in South Africa. One of them, Desmond Tutu, is Anglican Archbishop of Johannesburg; another, Franck Chikane, has just succeeded Dr Beyers Naude—Nobel Peace prize winner like Desmond Tutu—as Secretary General of the South African Council of Churches. Another, Simon Maimela, is now pan-African co-ordinator of the Ecumenical Association of Third World Theologians. It is enormously significant that in the slanderous campaign recently orchestrated by a French review—the *Figaro* magazine—against Liberation theology, the targets in South Africa of its journalists should have been chosen not from among the township chapels, but among the highest ranking church officials: Dr Beyers Naude, Nobel Peace prize winner, at that time Secretary General of the South African Council of Churches, and Dr Alan Boesak, President of the World Alliance of Reformed Churches and one of the founding fathers of the *Association Oecuménique des Théologiens Africains*. They were caricatured as being the pioneers of Christ-Marxist ecumenism.[12] Without realising it, perhaps, the

Figaro magazine illustrated the fact that the Liberation struggle in South Africa is from now on the affair of the official churches.

3. SOUTH AFRICAN THEOLOGICAL REASONING

The basic problem in South Africa is race. And race is defined by colour. The basic problem of South African Black theology is therefore also race and colour since race and colour determine all sectors of political, economic, social, cultural and religious life, falsifying the Bible, prostituting the gospels, dividing the churches and sowing hatred and conflict everywhere, the first objective of South African Liberation theology is the destruction of racism and the infernal system which stems from it: apartheid.

So the Bible appears as one of the basic sources of Black South African theological reasoning. It is the revealed Word of God: it tells us who is man and who is God. In the Bible man is created in God's image: black, white, yellow, red, all are free and equal, in the image of God. Biblical anthropology is poles apart from the anthropology of apartheid.

The God of the Bible, of Exodus, the books of history, the prophets, the psalms, the books of wisdom and the gospels, is a liberating God and saviour, who protects the poor, the weak and the oppressed against the oppressor, the rich and the powerful. In South Africa the God of the Bible can only be on the side of the oppressed, namely the Blacks.

In the gospels, the Son of God, through the mystery of his incarnation, took on the complete human condition: all are one in him. There are no longer either Jews or Pagans; we should add there are no longer either whites or blacks. Apartheid is a veritable apostasy of the Gospels. The good news of the Gospel brings the kingdom of God, the kingdom of the Beatitudes, which is a kingdom of justice and love. Apartheid, on the contrary, is a system of hatred, injustice and oppression. How can we build the kingdom of God when faced with such a system? What Christian meaning, what concrete reality is represented by power, revolution, violence, reconciliation?

As we see, it means nothing less than a contextualised African reading of the Bible. South African theological reasoning is confronted by a sea of iniquity, lies and violence. How can God's plan of salvation be seen through such opaqueness? That was the question asked in 1971 by the group of pastors who signed the open letter on nationalism, national-socialism and Christianity. It was the question taken up again, in September 1985, by the theologians, laymen, church officials, who signed the Kairos document. The image of the South African Christian people, divided, compliant, hesitating, with only a small core of unconditionally committed opponents of apartheid, is present in both documents, the open letter of 1971 and Kairos in 1985.

The African reading of the Bible, in South Africa, is in every sense of the word a liberating reading, for the oppressed race and for the word of God, itself captive and in chains. Since the founding of the Independent Churches in the last century, this reading can be said to have passed from the mythological syncretism of people like Isaiah Shembe of the Zulus, of Mwana Lesa or Bushiri (Taroki), of the Kumu of Zaïre, to the prophetic interpretation of the signs of the times and the dramatic calls for action of the Kairos document.

Reading of the Bible leads inevitably to the problem of humanity. The stake in South Africa is fairly and squarely the conception of humanity. The anthropological problem cannot be avoided. Anthropology is culture in the African sense of the word, that is to say the conception of humanity, the world and God. It was long though in the Liberation struggles in South Africa that culture was not of primary importance. Opinions have changed.[14] Wherever oppression begins by denying the identity and human dignity of its victims, the struggle for freedom must begin by the affirmation of that identity and that dignity. That is the struggle for cultural freedom. After placing African Liberation theology in its chronological framework, and defining its regional and cultural characteristics with reference to anglophone Africa, francophone Africa or South Africa, let us now return to the global project of African Liberation theology as defined by the Accra Declaration.

4. THE SOURCES OF AFRICAN THEOLOGY

The Accra Declaration mentions five sources of African theology. It is an indicative rather than an exhaustive list. These five sources are: the Bible, traditional religion, African anthropology, the Independent Churches and the African cultural heritage.

The Bible: African theologians know that the Bible is the word of God revealed to all men. They approach the Bible as believers. Their basic problem is that of an African reading of the Bible. An African reading looks for what God, through the Bible, has to say to the African people today about their life and destiny, in their context and situation of weakness, poverty and oppression. Such a reading discovers the word of God to be a message of salvation and freedom addressed to every man and every race. The God of the Bible is the God of the weak and the oppressed, as we have seen in considering South Africa. It is important to emphasise that the African reader neither adds to nor subtracts anything from the Bible. He simply adheres to the essential truth of the word of God. The liberating God of the Bible, he has not put him there, he has found him there. The same applies to the message of salvation and freedom. It is the very essence of the word of God. That is why the African reading of the Bible is also a fight for the freedom of the word of God, held captive and disfigured by the reading of the oppressors.

The African reading of the Bible is also a critical and scientific reading. The African theologians have undertaken a vast programme of research in this direction. In April 1972, in Jerusalem, they organised their first Congress on *The Bible and Black Africa*. The proceedings of this Congress were published.[14] A Second Congress has just taken place in Cairo on the same theme.[15] The Bible is a written document whose Mosaic origins are to be found in Africa. It is a document closely linked to the history not only of Israel, but of many races, and the Black races have an important place: for example, the marriage of Moses (Numbers 12). The Bible is also linked to the archaeology, the linguistics and history of the religions of the Near East. At no moment, at no period in ancient history, has Africa, Black Africa, been completely absent from these religions. It was also at Alexandria in Egypt that the Bible was, for the first and only time in antiquity, translated into a profane, non-semitic language. It was at Alexandria that Philo the Jew founded the allegorical exegesis and the simple exegis, in the modern sense of the word. It can be said that the first contextualised reading of the Bible was an African reading by the masters of Alexandria. The Bible raises other worrying problems. The concepts of *race, chosen people, covenant*, can be extrapolated, twisted and manipulated to the advantage of oppressors. This is effectively what has happened in order to justify all racism and all systems of domination and oppression. All these concepts now have to be examined closely by a critical African reading. This is one liberation process of the word of God. We must never forget that the Bible, taken as a whole, has a meaning: it is the message of salvation and freedom for the weak, the poor, the oppressed. It is through this meaning that the rest of the Bible makes sense, and consequently also the concepts of race, chosen people and covenant ... They translate God's preferential option for the weak, the poor, the oppressed with whom Israel is identified, not in an exclusive way, nor even in a normative way, but paradigmatically, to serve as an example. The transition from the dialectic of Jew and pagan to the dialectic of master and slave is a deception which must be demolished.

The concepts of *race, chosen people* and *covenant* are biblical realities all the more complex as they have been the object of countless manipulations. An African reading must exorcise them, demythologise and rid them of mystery, free them and restore them to their original function and meaning. Such a task demands a re-reading, not only of the revealed Word of God, but also of the whole of Western civilisation and its venture to dominate the world, a venture more menacing than every today because it is entering a cosmic and apocalyptic phase.

It would be quite wrong to believe that an African reading of the Bible just happens. It is an immense programme of research requiring time, and embracing questions as difficult as the African origins of Mosaic monotheism, the liberating function of religion in the political, economic, social and cultural spheres, or the contribution of Africa to the spiritual renewal of humanity today and tomorrow . . . etc.

The African Religions constitute, with the Bible, one of the major sources of African theology. The questions which are at the centre of traditional African religions are certainly not those of a discourse on God. The God of African monotheism is a God who is worshipped only in silence. Human chatter is dumb before the ineffable mystery of God. On the other hand, African religious reasoning concerns the fate of man, the struggle in each of us between life and death, and the final victory of life over death. The African religions, then, are religions of salvation. The initiation rites are the search for a universal way of salvation, leading to the victory of life over death. The whole universe is a vast battlefield where the battle of life and death is fought, and the initiation teaches man to read the names of life's allies in the great book of the cosmos, and to mobilise them against the adversary: death. Humanity is torn between the camp of life and the camp of death, and the basis of moral action lies in the choice between the two camps.

It is easy to understand why the religious praxis in traditional Africa is completely centred on the life of man and his *raisons d'être*: health, disease, birth, death, survival, the other world, fortune, misfortune, fertility, offspring, family, the community, success, failure, and finally harmony between the members of the community, and harmony between man and the cosmos.

Consequently one can understand the importance of the ritual which is the cosmic celebration of man's religious experience.

The traditional religions provide the African theologians with the basic structures of African religious experience; the categories and concepts which take account of the intelligibility of this experience and which weave the thread of all strictly religious reasoning. The good news of Jesus Christ as a message of freedom and salvation, and therefore as a strictly religious message, can only reach the African soul by using the language that the people can understand.

However, it is important to draw attention to certain fundamental aspects of the traditional African religions. Although it is true that they are religions of salvation, the ways of salvation are not always the same. The convention known as *ancestor worship* is a celebration of consanguinity and family life. The way to salvation here is a *via communis* leading to the fulfilment and the culmination of life shared in the family between the living and the dead. When we speak of inculturation, we must never forget that, at this level, the transition from the natural biological family to the family of grace and of union with God, does not occur without problems. The question is not that of the natural and the supernatural. Far from it! The question is the unavoidable one, which African tradition had very well observed: the question of same and other, of own and other people's, of kinsman and stranger. The transition from the order of kinship to the order of affiliation or adoption is common to mystery cults and all initiation systems. In ancestor worship the way of salvation leads to fidelity and identification with the ancestor. In mystery calls and initiation systems fidelity and identification are aimed at the other being, the stranger, the benevolent and liberating model who must come from elsewhere. The initiate must destroy the old man to reach the status of new man. He must pass through death to enter into the real life; he must change his name, speak another language, become a new man. At this level, the problems of Christian conversion and inculturation appear particularly relevant. Christology, soteriology, African spirituality can then espouse an authentically African reasoning, without betraying the mystery of man's meeting with the other being in whom he fulfils and completes himself.

African Anthropology: In my essay on African anthropology,[16] I emphasised some important aspects of the African conception of the human being. I do not wish to repeat that here. I would simply like to recall a few major points.

(a) The starting point of the Bantu philosophy is not the state of being in itself, but life. Life itself is not a simple reality; it is always perceived as the positive role of the life-death tension. It is this tension which fashions human existence in its profound reality. It is human existence which is the real object of wisdom, religion, social, political and cultural institutions, in short, what we call culture and civilisation.

(b) The human being has two dimensions: Man-Woman. In their complementarity, these two dimensions constitute the human period. The individual is not a person, but is on the way to personalisation. Man without woman is nothing; woman without man is nothing. Put the two together, and you will have a person in the African sense of the word. The couple thus defined appears as the principle, the image and the cosmic accomplishment of the human species. Within this reality lies the problem of Woman, not a problem in herself, but the solution to all problems. Society, history, all political, economic, social, cultural and religious institutions, are in the image of Man in his double man-woman dimension, and in his triple dimension father-mother-child.

This dialectic of the *monad* (individual), *dyad* (man-woman) and *triad* (father-mother-child) orders the whole African conception of moral action which is not only related to social and community life but also cosmic. The human person is not only dyad and triad, it is also cosmic, solidly bonded to the totality of the cosmic, to the spiritual universe by its soul, to the material universe by its body. It shares a common destiny with the world, is saved or lost with it.

Such an anthropology casts light on a host of major theological questions.

— the transition of the ethics of the individual to the ethics of the person and the community . . .
— theological reasoning on the Incarnation, considered not as a limited event, but as the assumption by the Son of God of the whole human nature and condition in their cosmic, anthropological and historic dimensions.
— the ecclesiology of the mystic body of Christ, as the living experience of Christ incarnate in the totality of human nature and history.
— the theology of ritual and the sacrament as a manifestation and celebration of the cosmic dimension of the incarnation of the Son of God, experienced symbolically in the Sign and its meaning.

The triadic conception of the human person is said to be the basis of ancestor worship and certain African theologians do not hestitate to present the role of Christ in the salvation process as that of proto-ancestor.

But the path of initiation best explains the mystery of the transition from death to true life, from the condition of sin to the condition of grace, from the status of son of condemnation to the status of son of God. Here it is the 'other being', the Son of God, who becomes nothing in order to become one of us, so that with him we can become sons of God. In a way which may be more widely comprehensible, the initiation mystery of Osiris or of Lyangombe foreshadows the mystery of salvation, of the meeting of man with God, of the victory of life over death in Jesus Christ.

The Independent Churches: We approach the question of the Independent

Churches as a theological *locus*. It is not necessary to re-examine their origins or even to propose them as models to be reproduced. The Independent Churches are in fact the direct fruits of the failure of oppressive Christianity. We cannot either perpetuate oppressive Christianity or repeat its failures. But the objective study of the historical phenomenon of the Independent Churches has a theological *locus*.

The context which gave birth to these churches offers, in fact, the model of the context of oppression, injustice and domination. Even more than the exile and enslavement of Egypt, racism and colonialism in Africa have allowed the most under-privileged of our peoples to reach an understanding, from within, of the mystery of God's liberating intervention in human history, the mystery of the Exodus. This is what the Independent Churches are desperately trying to experience. In a radical way, they pose the basic questions of the dignity of man made in the image of God, of the incarnation of the Son of God, of the universality of salvation in Jesus Christ, of the Church, mystical body of Christ . . .

It is not only by the questions they raise that the Independent Churches have a theological *locus*, but also by their attempts to answer them. It is clear in fact that independent churches, in the minds of the faithful, do not mean separate or schismatic churches, or sects, but the ideal form of the Church of Jesus Christ as a place of freedom, of fulfilment, and of confession of faith in Jesus Christ, in the freedom and dignity which they have at last found. The Church of Jesus Christ, the Universal Church, can only be that. We have seen above how the first African founders of Independent Churches sought in vain to find a legitimate place within the world Christian community. So, in seeking to free the Church from the slavery of racism and colonial domination, the Independent Churches were dismissed from history, marginalised and confined to the most shameful ghettoes. The ecclesiological problem remains, more real than ever, because it is increased twofold by the ecumenical problem. The African reading of the Bible, the inculturation of the African heritage as an essential dimension in the universality of the Church, the problem of religious freedom in Africa, of African spirituality, these all constitute so many areas of debate opened up by the Independent Churches which cry out to the theologian. For it is the Universal Church which we have to build, not a tribal sect. We have to end Africa's absence from the stage of history. We have to come out of the ghetto, free and liberated, to complete the construction of the body of Christ which is the Church.

5. THE AFRICAN WOMAN

What is the place of the African woman in the feminist movement which is spreading, sometimes with striking effects, in the modern world? To ask the question in this way is surely the wrong way to ask it. If we are to believe the female African theologians at their meeting in Yaoundé from 3–9 August 1986, there is certainly no case for claiming a place in a movement launched without them, far away from them and far from the reality of their daily lives. It might be thought we were joking when we declared earlier that the African woman is not a problem, but the solution to all problems. This does not mean that she has no problems. To be the solution to other people's problems is to be the target for all problems; it is literally to carry the weight of all problems. A close look at traditional society and at the anthropology which forms its basis shows that woman, being the necessary second dimension of the human person, represents the victory of life over death. That is why she may be said to be the solution to all problems. The implications of such an anthropology are immense. This is unfortunately not the place to enlarge on this. We can, at the very least, guess why maternity and the ministry of life in all its ritualistic expressions best represent the feminine function in traditional Africa. The social, political, economic and cultural struggles of the African woman rest on more radical demands, precisely because of the spiritual depth and density of their stakes. For the destiny of woman is the destiny of man, the destiny of the race and the species inseparably linked to the destiny of the world.

In the African context, one cannot truly identify the man-woman relationship with the class struggle. And when African woman struggles today to claim her place in political, economic, social and cultural life, it is not so much to beat the man as to save her own masculine dimension, for she knows that an Africa with its feminine dimension severed has no future.

This allows a better understanding of the impact of the positions taken by the female African theologians. The Church which they received from the West, because it has not accepted woman in her rightful place as giver of life, is a monster without heart and lungs. At their meeting in Yaoundé from 3–9 August 1986, the female African theologians serenely opened the great debate on their place in the Church and in the town. During this whole week and, it may be said, under the guiding influence of the Holy Spirit, they tackled the problems of an ecclesiology of the People of God without exclusion or discrimination. Their modest conclusion is more a question: 'The experience of spiritual life shows that God speaks to all men without discrimination. Is this not an invitation extended to the Church to give women their rightful place in its structures?'[17] This question may be modest; it is inescapable like the very gaze of God.

CONCLUSION

The picture which we have just sketched of African theology is inevitably too brief, too incomplete, too cursory. In the first part, the phenomenon of African theology was presented within its dual chronological and geographical framework. That was necessary, because African theology is closely tied to the African history of the last hundred years. It is also linked to the geographic and cultural dispersion of our continent. The lack of communication between anglophone, arabophone and francophone Africans is to be regretted.

One can simply record the barriers of foreign languages, with their corollary, the cultural dissipation of the continent. So, on this point, our theological research is still conditioned by foreign cultures.

It was to overcome this obstacle that we created at Accra in 1977 the *Association Oecuménique des Théologiens Africians*. The programme of this association has served as a leading strand throughout this paper. It may be said that African theology now forms a united front consisting of South Africa, Madagascar, East Africa, Central Africa and West Africa. This attempt at unity and solidarity does not do away with regional or cultural diversities. In this paper, we have listed the themes and major sources of African theology. We also mentioned the methodological problems, especially concerning the analysis of the African context.

It has repeatedly been said that African theology is on the move. It is a programme of research which progresses from day to day. What is at stake is far more than just the continent of Africa. In reality, we are concerned with the whole Christian tradition which, thanks to African theology, is in the very process of reaching a new dimension of its universality.

Translated by Barrie Mackay

Notes

1. See Mgr Patrick Kalilombe 'Le thème de la libération dans la théologie africaine en pays anglophones' in *Documents interéglises*, April–June 1985 pp. 19–33.

2. For the bibliography of these authors refer to: Ngindu Mushete 'Bibliographie de Théologie africaine' in *Bulletin de Théologie africaine*, especially vol. VI, no. 12, July–December 1984 pp. 390–399 and in the subsequent numbers.

3. Sheik Anta Dop, after *Nation Nègre et culture* (1956), published in quick succession: *L'Afrique Noire prècoloniale* (1960), *Les fondements culturels, techniques et industriels d'un futur Etat fédéral d'Afrique Noire* (1960), *L'Unité culturelle de l'Afrique Noire* (1960).

4. On the publications of these authors see B. T. A., vol. VI, 11, 1984 pp. 141–151.

5. The work had first appeared in Flemish at Elisabethville in the Belgian Congo.

6. In *Civilisation*, (Brussels) vol. 1, no. 3 pp. 54–63.

7. Brussels *Académie Royale des sciences coloniales* (Extracts). The complete text was published the following year, in 1956.

8. These were the authors:

V. Mulago 'Necessité de l'adaptation missionnaire chez les Bantu du Congo', and 'Le Pacte du sang et la communion alimentaire, pierre d'attente de la communion eucharistique'.

J. Thiam 'Du clan tribal à la communauté chrétienne.'

J. C. Bajeux 'Mentatlité noire et mentalité biblique.'

E. Verdieu & P. Ondia 'Sacerdoce et Négritude.'

G. Bissainthe 'Catholicisme et indigénisme religieux.'

R. Dosse & R. Sastre 'Propogande et verité.'

R. Sastre 'Liturgie romaine et négritude.'

Meinrad Hebga 'Christianisme et négritude'.

Alexis Kagame 'La littérature orale au Rwanda.'

J. Parisot 'Vaudou et christianisme.'

9. See *Revue du clergé africain*, no. 15, July 1960 pp. 333–352, 'Débat sur la théologies africaine.' Canon Vanneste's contribution is on pages 346–352 entitled 'D'abord une vraie théologie.'

10. F. Grahay 'Le décollage conceptuel, condition d'une philosophie bantu.' (*Diogène*, no. 52 pp. 61–84).

—K. Matthews 'Can Christianity survive in Africa?' (*Ministry*, no. 5 pp. 97–98).

—F. Murray 'The Church is universal.' (AFER, vol. 7 pp. 328–336).

—J. Poulton 'Post – christian Africa.' (AFER, vol. 7 pp. 75–76).

11. On this publications of these authors, and on the bibliography of this period, consult the *Bulletin de Théologie Africaine*, vol. VI, no. 11 pp. 141–151 and vol. VI, no. 12 pp. 391–415.

12. *Figaro Magazine*, Saturday 17 October, and Saturday 24 October 1987, Exclusive enquiry entitled, 'La Faucille et la Croix.' (The Sickle and the Cross).

13. cf. Patrick A. Kalilombe 'Le thème de la Libération dans la Théologie africaine en pays anglophones' in *Documents interéglises*, 1985 p. 29.

14. Prof. Engelbert Mveng & Prof Zwi Werblowsky *L'Afrique Noire et la Bible* (Jerusalem, Israel Interfaith Committee 1974).

15. 'Africa and the Bible', Cairo, Egypt, 14–21 August 1987. This Congress was organised by the *Association Oecuménique des Théologiens Africains*.

16. In *L'Afrique dand l'Eglise, Paroles d'un Croyant*, pp. 7 et seq. The proceedings of the Symposium organised at Abidjan by the Insitut Catholique de L'Afrique de l'Ouest (ICAO) on 'African religious experience and interpersonal relations' (16–20 September 1980) may also consulted. Special edition of *Savanes et Forêts* 1982.

17. Conclusion of the final report of the Meeting of African Women Theologians (Yaoundé, 3–9 August 1986). This meeting was organised by the Ecumenical Association of Third World Theologians (EATWOT).

Tissa Balasuriya

Emerging Theologies of Asian Liberation

THOUGH CHRISTIANITY is Asian in origin, in modern times it has been regarded as an alien faith in most of Asia except in South India and the Middle East which have Churches coming down from apostolic times.

The traditional Catholic and Protestant Churches in Asia share some general characteristics. Western in origin, they did not contest the Western exploitation of Asia. The traditional theology of these Churches aimed at the conversion of 'unbelievers' to the Christian faith which was considered the unique or safe path to eternal salvation. Hence an attitude of superiority towards other religions and a disregard and disrespect for their rites, traditions, literature, places of worship, sages and founders.

This theological position prevailed in the Catholic and Protestant Churches for many centuries from the time the Western missions to the East began after the voyages of Vasco da Gama. The Christians were generally kept away from the persons of other religions—in a relatively ghetto-ish existence.

Everywhere in Asia Christians are a small minority except in the Philippines. They are also often sociological minorities in that the missionaries went more readily to the marginalised groups such as a minority race, caste or tribe within each country. This further strengthened their minority consciousness, defensive apologetic mentality and dependence on the clergy and the 'mother' churches of the West.

The churches were very intensely dedicated to social service to the sick, orphans and the needy. This was the practical expression of their love of

God: and love of neighbour taught by Jesus. The schools of the Christian churches have won warm recognition and sometimes envy, in all the Asian countries. These services did not however radically contest the Asian exploitative feudal and colonial structures, though a few national leaders emerged from these schools.

A significant change has been taking place in the Asian churches during the last two to three decades. It was prepared by Western scholars and creative Asian thinkers from the last century. They were groping for ways in which Christianity and Christians could be more genuinely Asian and open to all human values. The transformation in the Catholic Churches principally around the World Council of Churches, opened the way for Asian Christians to become more incarnate in our cultures and countries and participate in the processes of human liberation at both a personal and societal level.

The contemporary renewal of the Churches in Asia has been as elsewhere—motivated by new theological insights. These perspectives have brought up a new generation of Christian faithful and leaders. Cardinal Kim of Seoul and Cardinal Sin of Manila are powerful personalities who represent this trend of active Christian commitment to the service of their peoples. The Christian human rights activists in South Korea, the Philippines, India, Malaysia, Singapore, Sri Lanka, Taiwan, Pakistan, Bangladesh are now a growing body in the Asian countries.

In China the Christians live in post-revolutionary societies. After decades of difficulties they are now coming to a new modus vivendi with Marxist socialist regimes. They are socialistic in socio-economic options, post-denominational in inter-Church relations and endeavour to be self-reliant in management, finance, personnel and doctrinal and theological evolution. The conflict between the Chinese Catholic Patriotic Church and the Vatican is still unresolved, though the relationships have been improving in recent years.

Gradually Christians are evolving in all the Asian countries from being scared spectators of the radical changes in their societies to participants in these processes even though it be in small groups. The Edsa experience of the Philippines in February 1986 was, of course, a high water mark of Christian presence as a force for freedom. It was an indication that decades of patient effort at the transformation of the Christians was beginning to bear fruit. It is likely to have a great impact on the whole of Asia and the world as a revelation of the potential of 'People's Power' in determining some crucial issues of public life.

These trends are leading many Christians to join small groups of people's movements of students, youth, workers, women, tribals, outcastes, different oppressed groups and intellectuals who opt for a more just society. These are the creative nuclei in the Asian Churches. They work with persons and groups of similar orientation though of different beliefs and persuasions. They are at the frontiers of change and sometimes face much opposition and misunderstanding and even martyrdom.

1. METHODOLOGY OF THEOLOGICAL REFLECTION

More recent Asian theological development includes a two-fold approach in addition to the acceptance of the scientific attitudes developed in Europe and North America.

First, use of *social analysis* leading to an option on behalf the poor. This has been partly the influence of the Asian context including Marxist societies and parties and partly the influence of Latin American liberation theology:

A second methodology is inter-religious dialogue that led to rethinking of Christianity in its dogmas and practices. The study, research and contemplation are part of the methodology. This two influences the liturgy, architecture and life style of Christians.

This meant having two further principal sources for theologising in addition to the Bible and Christian tradition: the social reality and the religious character of the people. Hence the *peoples* situation, aspirations and struggles and the teachings of the founders of the religions, their sacred writings, and popular religious experiences are also sources for Asian Christian theology. The *peoples* experience include particularly those of the poor and the oppressed including women.

Thus the *subject doing theology* becomes the human group engaged in such dialogue and commitment and reflecting in a contemplative manner on their situation and action. The Asian philosophies, in which the religious thoughts are expressed also influence Christian theology in its more theoretical interpretations. In practical life the values that are common to the religions are becoming the basis of meditation and action in society concerning human rights, freedom, justice and peace.

The languages of the different peoples and the art forms such as poetry— are used for expressing the theological reflections that emerge from these situations. The dialogue of life—of living with persons of other religions, sharing their life style of poverty and participating in their struggles—is one of the most potent influences on theological reflection.

The more creative theologians are those who have been involved in action-reflection with *peoples* movements and/or in inter-religious dialogue. The Chinese Christian re-thinking after the Revolution involves a methodology of self-reliance in the *three self movement*: Self-reliance in *management*, in *resources* and in *doctrine*. In a sense they go back to the experience of the early Church as a theological basis of their point of view as in the local Catholic Church choosing its Bishops.

The Bible in this background is accepted as one major source of theology, but not the sole source. Further it is one which needs to be complimented and even corrected in that it comes from one particular ethnic tradition, is generally written by males and has been interpreted by Christians. It is inadequate for the Asian Context as there is much in it that is ethnocentric and exclusivist. Christian tradition as a source of theology has also to be similarly evaluated, and where necessary corrected.

2. MAIN CREATIVE THEMES OF THEOLOGY IN ASIA

Response to Asian Poverty

Asian Christian theological reflection on poverty has several strands. One has been the accentuation of the identification with the poor in life style as in the ashramic movement in India. It includes an effort at identifying with the poorest of the poor, the tribals, dalits, outcastes. From this tradition has grown a deep contemplative reflection on the identification of God with the poor, and the formation of action groups that espouse the cause of exploited groups. This trend has been generally universal in Asia. Many theological writings have been influenced by a close contact with the very poor. Kim Chi Ha in Korea, Kosuke Koyama writing from Thailand, Carlos Abesamis, Ed de La Torre, Julio Labayen in the Philippines, Samuel Rayen, Sebastian Kappen, Amalorpavadass in India, Aloy Pieris, Michael Rodrigo and others in Sri Lanka, are a few examples.

Marxism and Latin American liberation theology have also influenced the analysis of poverty with a consciousness of exploitation and an emphasis on a radical change of social structures. There are cross-currents of views and options in the context of different groups such as those who have opted for an armed struggle and for socialistic solutions, and others emphasising non-violent processes of social change. In the Philippines gradually the consciousness of the relevance of the Christian culture for resistance to exploitation and oppression has brought a close relationship between religion and the struggle against poverty due to exploitation.

The struggle of the more socially committed Christian groups in *South Korea* has been against the repressive regimes backed by the US military presence. Theologians have developed the powerful concepts of the suffering dominated people, the 'minjung', to whom God has promised liberation.

Minjung theology links up social analysis, biblical exegesis and liberative practice to develop this theological reflection in South Korea. Still others emphasise the need to press for the reunification of North and South Korea as a priority for the Korean people's future. The Korean theologians are very active locally and nationally. They are ecumenical in linking across Christian denominations.

In India the theological reflection on poverty has been marked by the depth and extent of poverty in the vast subcontinent which has also very rich industrial magnates, landlords and even remnants of Maharajahs. Though profound in reflection, Christian groups have not been able to make so significant a contribution to the national causes as in the Philippines and South Korea. In India and most countries of South and South-East Asia there is a great consciousness of the impact of other religions and of the need of articulating liberative thought concerning poverty in the context of these religions.

The theological reflection and social action of small groups in Malaysia and Singapore have recently led to repression by their Governments. In Singapore liberation theology is charged with subversion. Recently the Christian Conference of Asia (CCA) offices were summarily closed down and all foreigners working there expelled. Sixteen Christians—mainly Catholics—were imprisoned on charges of being Communist. Vincent Cheng, considered a leader among them, is still in prison. In Malaysia Bro. Anthony Rogers is likewise in prison. These are indications of how small groups that have not written many theological books have been envolving their own theology and praxis to the extent of being considered a danger by the ruling establishment in countries where Christians are a tiny minority in the population.

There are some theological writers who have, in addition to critiquing capitalism, espoused more radical alternatives as Geevarghese Mar Ostrathios in his *Theology of a Classless Society*. Chinese theologians such as K. H. Ting reflect in the background of what he calls a post-liberation situation. Here a more egalitarian society has been set up and the effort of Christian theologians is to help in its development by bringing the Churches to support it, while exercising or demanding religious freedom, and being conscious of the limitations of the new society. In Vietnam too similar trends have developed of Christians supporting the socialist pattern despite the difficulties the country faces.

The *planetary dimension* of the issues of justice and poverty are clearer in Asia than in the rest of the world due to the extent and vastness of proverty and the enormous population contained in the Asian countries. 'Planetary Theology' takes the world as the locus for theologising and places Asia's future in the context of global changes in economic as well as political structures.

The inspiration for this theologising is in a re-appraisal of the life and teaching of Jesus and the understanding of God as caring for all. All the elements that have contributed towards a renewal of theology in the direction of the Church of the poor are also present in Asian countries such as re-reading of the Bible and of Church history from the point of view of the poor, re-thinking the life and mission of the Jesus of Mary and of the nature of the Church.

Dialogue with other Religious and Asian Culture

After gradual beginnings of openness, helped in part by modern European missionaries, there is now a veritable theological explosion in this field. Asian responses are varied in relation to the religions and cultures. There are Churches and theologians who are specially concerned with Asian Art and architecture, for example, Takenaka of Japan, Jothi Sahi of India. Some are steeped in linguistic and philosophical studies. Among these some have contributed to profound theological reflection such as Raymundo Panniker and Aloy Pieris.

There are different levels of inter religious dialogue: dialogue of intellectual discourse and study; dialogue in worship and liturgy; dialogue of life—living together and relating to society at different levels; dialogue while participating in the people's struggle for life.

All these have contributed to Christian theology. The Asaramic movement, Zen meditation and revival groups in different countries have developed interreligious dialogue at the level of a deep inner experience of communion among believers of different persuasions and primordial religious experiences, seem to lead towards a togetherness in relating to transcendent values and to the Absolute. Some have developed this line of meditation in the direction of commitment to social justice, for example, Ruben Habito: *Total Liberation—Zen Spirituality and the Social Dimension* (Maule 1986).

Contemplation leading to commitment, and commitment being nourished by contemplation are distinct Asian emphases. Amalor-pavadass has developed this line of action—reflection—action at his Ashram in Mysore. Hindu, Buddhist, Islamic contemplative experiences have influenced Asian Christian theology and spirituality.

The development of Asian liturgies, including Eucharistic services is another specific Asian contribution to Christian living that is the fruit of Asian theological reflection in the context of other religions. The Indian liturgy and the Workers Mass developed by the Christian Workers' Fellowship in

Sri Lanka are two noteworthy developments. The sacred scriptures of the other religions are being used increasingly in Christian meditation and worship. An even more dynamic development is the dialogue of life in which Christians live with persons of other religions, learn the religions together and relate to the people's problems. There are numerous action groups engaged in such a level of experience. Michael Rodrigo who was martyred last November in Buttala in the interior of Sri Lanka was a theologian who thus identified with the poorest of the poor in life style and social commitment.

There are groups of Asian Christians who work together with persons and groups of other religions for the human and societal liberation of their people. Such experiences are now growing in almost all the countries of Asia. They base their actions on the common core of values that are shared by the religions. Today hardly any large scale action for justice, peace and freedom takes place among Christians in Asia without an openness to similar groups of other religions. The Philippines may be an exception in so far as it is largely Christian in religious application. Most Asian theologians of liberation are tending in this direction. Aloy Pieris has been a pioneer in articulating the close inter-relation of Asian poverty and Asian religiosity as two poles for a theology of liberation in Asia.

Sebastian Kappen is strongly critical of the establishments of Society and of the Church—based on a sharp social critique. He has been more open to the ideology of Marxism than are most Asian theologians. In China the evolution of theology is now opening towards the other religions in their post-liberation experience. They see the linkage between the values of Chinese culture and the liberated China that has thus been spared some of the evils of Western capitalistic culture.

The impact of Asian culture is seen also in the forms of writing and in the sensitiveness in reflection. C. S. Song in 'Third Eye Theology' develops the theme that the Asian mode of theologising is and can be influenced by the Asian way of living that is open to nature, seeks harmony and is reflective or introspective. Much of such writing with theological import is in the form of short stories, poems, plays etc., and are in the Asian languages.

Another contribution to theology is the development of the concept and practice of the pluralist human group or community as the basic unit of action—reflection. In most of Asia the 'base Christian Community' would be a concept that is narrow, and limiting in relation to the reality of a plural and even secular society.

Corresponding to the growth of women's movements there has been the development of theology from *a feminist perspective*. While this trend has benefitted much from the North American and European feminist writings, the Asian poverty and religious need. Asian women generally view their struggles within the wider human struggle of both women and men in their countries. They are very important participants in the *peoples* movements all over Asia specially in developing non-violent methods for social change.

The dimensions of contemplation, compassion, wholeness and harmony which are noteworthy in the Asian background influence the Asian feminist action—reflection, while they are conscious of the long term marginalisation of women in Asia. Among the more significant contributions are those of Marianne Katoppo *Compassionate and Free* (Geneva 1979) and of many writers in *In God's Image* published by the Christian Conference of Asia. The Catholic women religious who are about a 100,000 in Asia are now laying the intellectual and experiential bases for a significant future thrust towards a theology that is Asian, Christian, dialogical, liberational and feminist.

Far Reaching Issues

The experience and renewal of Christianity in Asia is bringing to the fore some very far reaching questions. Asian theology shares with the rest of the Third World the critique of the Western Euro − North American theology. Beyond these and the general feminist critique there are specific issues arising from the multi-religious context, the extreme poverty, the massive populations and the experiences of Marxist regimes specially in China.

The crucial issues are in relation to the nature of the Absolute, divine revelation, the sources of theology, the person of Jesus, the role of the Christ, the nature of the human predicament—the 'fall', original sin, redemption in Jesus, grace, the mission of the Church, Christian liturgy, proclamation witness and dialogue, justice within nations and world justice.

The traumatic experience of Christianity in Asia makes present day theologians question radically some positions which are taken for granted in most of the rest of world Christianity. The consciousness of the Church having blundered during several centuries in Asia in its failure to see God's presence in other faiths brings about an understandable and radical questioning by Asian theologians. They are increasingly suspicious the very presuppositions on which the Western construct of Christian theology has been built up over centuries.

Concerning *revelation* many Asian theologians—particularly in India and Sri Lanka—hold that God need not be limited to the Bible in her/his revelation to humanity. The sacred texts of other religions can be source of divine revelation. At the same time both these and the Bible need to be studied critically to exclude elements which cannot be from God—such as an excessive ethnocentricism or 'religionism' (a concept developed by the present writer in *Planetary Theology*). God has spoken to all the peoples of the world in diverse ways and continues to do so today too. This raises a major hermeneutical issue concerning the nature of revelation, the sources of theology and their interpretation.

The non-theistic thinking of Theravada Buddhism, and the pantheistic perceptions in Hinduism, influence Asian Christian theologians to search for deeper meaning concerning the nature of the Absolute. The affirmations concerning *God*, the *creation* of the universe, the beginning of human life and life beyond death are being rethought in the dialogue with other religions (and secular ideologies). Theologians see that what can be said concerning the divine nature is so relative to our human experience and philosophical schools. Alternative interpretations are possible concerning human knowledge of the Transcendent and about the relationship of God to human life.

The story of the Fall of the first parents leading to the alienation of the whole of humanity from the destiny for which God created the human race is questioned by Asian theologians who find this a particular interpretation given by writers like Paul and later developed in Western Europe. When *original sin* in its traditional presentation as in the Council of Trent is thus questioned the basic concepts of redemption and of mission of the Church also need to be re-thought. In what sense did Jesus redeem humanity? Are the other religions salvific through their ministrations? What is the role of the human conscience in determining a person's eternal destiny? These are currently being discussed not only by theologians but also by ordinary persons in our countries as they live in a plural environment in which there are people of good will (and otherwise) in all faith traditions.

An even more vital issue is concerning the nature and person of Jesus the Christ. Jesus is warmly appreciated in his compassion and struggle for human liberation as seen in the gospels. Some Asian theologians are quite sceptical of the meaningfulness of Christological definitions as in the Council of Chalcedon that Christ is one person in two natures. These are presentations that, in any case, are not intelligible since they deal with the nature of the divinity that the human mind cannot comprehend. Further they are seen as stumbling blocks in the context of Islam with its affirmation of God not being a mortal human being, and of the claims of other religions concerning their own founders and seers. The issue is in what way can we understand Jesus as God, and how does this impinge on his humanity.

The Christ as cosmic is acceptable in the context of the acknowledgment of a universal Absolute—an 'Atman Braham'. How this Christ is incarnated in Jesus in an exclusive manner is a problem in the background of several possible manifestations (avatars) of the divine.

The nature of *redemption* is another critical issue—redemption from what? This depends on the presupposition of original sin. The concept of the mission of the Church has already been adjusted by the world Churches, specially under pressure, from reflections from the Afro-Asian context. Christian *mission* is now seen as primarily for the transformation of persons and societies according to the values of the Kingdom of God presented by Jesus. In this service the Gospel is borne witness to. Conversion as such is not the goal of Christian mission as salvation can take place in and through other religions also. Conversions to any religion are welcome when they are free, genuine and authentic.

The Church encourages all to live authentic lives according to one's religion, while those freely wishing to be Christians are welcome. The *divisions within Christianity* are importations into Asia of the results of quarrels among European Christians, and hence inter-Christian ecumenism is now developing well in the theological search.

Asian theology is pointing out quite clearly that the Church while not being essential for human salvation has a role and responsibility for humanising the world. One of its principal tasks has to be (re) conversion of Europeans and North-Americans to the Gospel of love and sharing announced by Jesus. The response to the demands for freedom, justice and peace in the pluralist troubled Asian context, within an unjust world order is the principal challenge to Asian theology and of Asian theology to the world Churches.

The exigencies of poverty and exploitation are pressing towards an emphasis on meaningfulness and relevance of teachings, liturgy and life. The Churches must become Churches of the poor, and the poor have to be a source and subject of theology. Asia's poor are about 97 per cent not of the Christian faith. How then is Christian theology to be shaped by their sorrowful human existence?

The pluralist environment is leading Asian Christian theologians to re-think and re-articulate the presentations of Christian dogma. This is leading to a greater *de-dogmatisation* and an insistent accent on the living of the basic moral and spiritual teachings concerning love of God and love of neighbour in an unjust world. In so far as Asian theologians respond authentically to the challenges of their situation they will be helping to evolve Christian theology in the direction of a Christian community that is less Church-centred and more human-centred, and hence more God-centred as Jesus himself was. Asian theologians are increasingly in favour of inter-religious meditation and communion in prayer. What is called *Com-*

municatio in Sacris is not such a problem provided the spirituality is genuine. Various experiences are developing in this direction.

This is a much more radical re-thinking of theology than has been hitherto undertaken in the Churches since the earliest centuries. The Church in that sense is opening up to a new view of a pluralist humanity in which all religions are challenged by their core spiritual values beyond the particularities of their historical origins. Humanity will then move unto an era in which God / the Absolute will be recognised and worshipped more in 'in Spirit and truth' than in any mere human organisation. In that sense the Asian Churches are bound to have a deep impact on Christian thought and hopefully action in the nineties and in the 21st century.

Julio de Santa Ana

The Situation of Latin American
Theology (1982–1987)

THERE IS no doubt that liberation theology is now the dominant theology in
Latin America. Since it first appeared theological debate has been conducted
around it. It is the indispensable reference point for any attempt to describe the
state of theology in Latin American countries. For the first time in Latin
American history this is a theology which succeeds in expressing with strength
and conviction the experience of a large number of Christian communities.
Although liberation theology does not command a majority, all who engage in
theological reflection do so in dialogue or polemic with it. I has managed to
articulate and systemise clearly those aspects of Christian life which best
express the faith of Latin American communities.

However the most striking thing about liberation theology is the
dynamism it has shown over the last few years. This can be seen in various
ways: the growing number of publications expressing the views of liberation
theology, and their reception by the public: books by liberation theologians
are quickly sold out and reissued in second and third editions within two
years' of publication. There are also numerous courses set up on its main
themes. It takes up a lot of space in the media. We are seeing a previously
unknown phenomenon: theology has become an important topic of
everyday conversation—at home, in the street and in cafes (not just in
church and university).

There are several reasons for this vitality. Firstly, there are the Latin
American ones. From its first appearance on the scene in the late sixties

liberation theology related to this context. From then on, the setting in which liberation theology continued to be done was in the practice of liberating faith by popular communities and other important sectors of Latin American society. As the Latin American situation, particularly in the Church, is a dynamic one, this is reflected – in their own way – in the work of liberation theologians.

During the last few years important things have happened in the history of Latin American countries. New strong people's movements have arisen, in particular among women, Indians and blacks. Here the people are irrupting into history as active subjects who wish to be the conscious protagonists of their own lives. Consequently the military domination of the sixties and seventies is not so much in evidence now. The armed forces, particularly in South America (with the exception of Chile and Paraguay) have ceased to govern their countries. Civilian governments have been restored. Christian communities have an important part in this process. Christians in people's organisations have defended and promoted human rights and supported other social and political demands. We need only look at what is happening in Central America, particularly El Salvador, where Christians are playing an important part in the people's struggle.

Of course the traditional oligarchies and those who represent the interests of international capital are not going to let the people advance without trying to stop them. Once again we can take Central America as an example. Those in power are massively resisting the people's movement. This results in intense social struggles, with war in both town and country.

In some Latin American countries there is a precarious balance of power between the opposing forces. The people's forces (in which Christians, as we said, are playing a major part) are fighting for democratic rights and institutions which would safeguard human rights. The reactionary organisations are responding with all their resources, influence and power, often very violently. In many cases the result of this tension has been a kind of 'controlled democracy', which does not satisfy the majority. This is a political set-up which might have suited Latin American societies thirty or forty years ago but which seems anachronistic today. The might of those with economic and military strength has carried more weight than all the people's spirit. This is a fragile and transitory situation. The question is what kind of democracy would suit Latin American societies today? This search influences the lives of the people's Christian communities and thereby has an effect on theology.

Hence a second reason for liberation theology's current dynamism is what is going on in the life of the Church. The Ecclesial Base Communities (EBCs) are growing in strength and numbers. Many more churches now give priority to pastoral programmes based in these EBCs. New church forms are also developing: the mission to the indigenous peoples of the continent, support for black communities, suburban women's groups etc. This dynamism in the Church gives liberation theology its power of renewal.

Just as in secular society, within the churches there are forces resisting and attacking these new trends. One of the most obvious manifestations of this opposition was the campaign against certain liberation theologians between 1983 and 1986. (In some cases it still continues.) This campaign created alliances between forces, institutions and groups in nearly all the churches. The starting point was the attack on liberation theology by the Document of the Sacred Congregation for the Doctrine of the Faith (published in August 1980 as a guideline for Reagan's administration.) Then negative judgments were pronounced against liberation theology from other quarters. Important ecclesiastical bodies were involved in this campaign. Some theologians were forced to submit to trial and sanctions.[1] Nevertheless they were able to count on the support of other important sectors in the churches, especially the EBCs and other church forms among the people. All this gave an enormous impetus to reflection by liberation theologians.

Thirdly, we should also mention reasons inherent in liberation theology itself and its own specific development. Liberation theologians in their Latin American setting developed and deepened their thinking. They had to cope with a campaign attacking their theology. This attack had two main groups of supporters. Conservative forces interested in defending their privileges and interests used the opportunity to have a go at those who had succeeded in inspiring the people to seek necessary changes. And ecclesiastical authorities employed mainly dogmatic arguments to try to discredit liberation theology.[2] Liberation theologians responded. This has meant that over the past few years Latin America has been the scene of lively theological debates. Liberation theology has proved its strength, creativity and maturity in this arena.

Of course a theology's dynamism is manifested not so much through its polemic but in the way it which it helps and inspires members of communities to strengthen their faith, carry on the Church's mission and fulfil Jesus' command to preach the gospel 'to the ends of the earth'. This mission and gospel-preaching is the *ekkliesia* turning outwards to the world and bearing *martyria* to its faith. Thus a theology is valid and efficacious when it helps Christian communities fulfil their mission and bear witness to Jesus Christ before the world, when it enables them to respond the world's challenges.

Liberation theologians have done this. They have shown that they are alert to the development of the Church's situation in the world, particularly in Latin America.

Firstly, we find an awareness among them of the need to respond to the expectations of *all* oppressed social groups in Latin America. It does not do to generalise about the poor. They have individual faces and their individuality should not be overlooked. Often they are country women, or women living on the outskirts of cities, the unemployed or under-employed, workers whose wages have gone down considerably in value over the last few years.[3] Indians whose nations have suffered oppression for almost five centuries, blacks who continue to assert their identity in the face of white racism. These individual faces of the poor challenge liberation theologians to develop new lines of thought and fill out their arguments with particular details.

Secondly, we find an awareness of the importance of *economic* factors. With the exception of the US, Latin America is the region in most debt in all the world. Because of this situation, if ways are not found to deal with this weight of debt, the future of Latin American countries is mortgaged for a long time to come. To this should be added the greed of transnational capital which dominates the economy of the region. The combination of both elements: foreign debt and the process of capital internationalisation—in fact they are closely connected—has caused the people of these countries to suffer great alienation and frustration. Economic growth has stagnated or even deteriorated, which has affected employment levels. Unemployment is growing. Because of their obligation to pay interest on the debt, these countries have to export as much as possible to obtain currency. This forces them to lower the price of their products to make them competitive in the international market. So of course they have to keep wages down. The poor are sacrificed to the contemporary version of Moloch. And this is justified by arguing the need to pay a 'social cost' for development. Liberation theologians have become aware of this challenge and begun to respond to it, as we shall see later.

Thirdly, political evolution and especially the search for new democratic forms allowing for more majority participation, have led many members of the EBCs to see the need for a political pastoral theology, more specifically on the tense relations between the practice of the faith and the practice of militancy, especially in political parties.[4] Another political challenge is the relationship with Marxist parties. This is the case of Christians in Cuba and Nicaragua, for example. A major event here was the publication of Frei Betto's book *Fidel and Religion*[5], which was a Latin American best seller in 1986 and 1987. The book considers the particular case of Cuba, where for the first time Marxists at highest government levels are expressing public concern over the question of religion.

Fourthly, the realisation of the importance of women[6], Indians and blacks in Latin American societies has led liberation theologians to pay more attention to these oppressed sectors, especially the *culturally* oppressed. More notice is being taken of these groups' traditional values, including religious values. This is not the first time anything like this has happened. Bartolomé de las Casas, Valdivieso and others did something similar in their preaching. The difference now is that we see the need to value these oppressed cultures more objectively. We understand in the religious cultures and traditions or these groups there are evangelical elements which cannot be ignored or despised. This had led liberation theologians to engage in new forms of ecumenical activity.[7]

This new awareness is confirming a tendency which was already visible by the mid-seventies: liberation theology is turning to specific issues. It is no longer possible to think of it as just discourse on how to do theology, or a reflection on method (contextual, inductive).[8] Shortly before the beginning of the eighties liberation theologians attempted to come up with a system covering the various aspects of theology. We can see this clearly in the collection *Teologia y Liberación* published simultaneously in Spanish and Portuguese.[9] This work was useful to the communities to help them deepen their own theological thinking. We have already noted some of the challenges confronting liberation theology. We have mentioned the dynamism of the EBCs and new church forms. Now we should list some of the specific areas in which liberation theologians are active.

First, there is a renewed interest in bible study. From its beginning liberation theology was a biblical theology. The central importance of study of God's Word in the EBCs has led to groups of biblical scholars from various Latin American countries meeting to work together. The results have come out in an important number of publications, which show the characteristic trends of biblical exegesis and hermeneutics in Latin America.[10] This biblical orientation is fundamental to liberation theology. It places it in direct contact both with the source of Christian revelation and with the living language of the communities. God and Church are the constant reference points for liberation theology.

Secondly, liberation theologians have often been criticised for paying too much attention to political issues. Some even add that liberation theology is just a social ethic. Those who take this line ignore the importance ascribed by liberation theologians to Christian *spirituality*.[11] Prayer and sacramental life are fundamental questions for liberation theology in understanding the character of Christian life. This attention to spirituality is very important to them.

Thirdly, although they started a decade ago, the work of the Commission for the Study of the History of the Church in Latin American (CEHILA) deserves special mention. For just over ten years this group has been doing systematic work in all the countries of the region. The group's common hermeneutic for understanding Church history in the area is the viewpoint of the poor and oppressed. The group's findings and contributions are extremely useful to Latin American theology.[12] And even more important, through this work the people's Christian communities gain a clearer sense of being themselves part of the Latin American historical process.

Fourthly, during the period we are considering, Latin American liberation theology has become more inclusive. The contributions of Beatriz Couch, Yvone Gebara, Elsa Tamez and others opened the way for other women theologians such as Maria Clara Bingemer, Tereza Cavalcanti, Nelly Ritchie, Ana Maria Tepedino and others. Their work is beginning to correct the excessively male bias in liberation theology until the beginning of this decade. Certainly the women's contribution is one of the most promising hopes for the future development of Latin American theology.[13]

Fifth, over the last five or six years the Christological character of liberation theology has been reaffirmed. To the works of Leonardo Boff[14] and Jan Sobrino,[15] we should add the valualble work of people like Juan Luis Segundo,[16] Benedito Ferraro[17] and the late lamented Hugo Echegaray.[18] This work finds an echo in the experience of the people's Christian communities. Their members see Jesus as the one who—through the power of the Holy Spirit—is with them and encourages them. Jesus is the model for the communities, their suffering, hopes and work. He is the constant reference point for their faith. Liberation theology makes this explicit both in its nourishing reflection on the historical Jesus, and its affirmation that it belongs to the tradition of the great creeds of the ecumenical councils of the Church's early centuries.

Sixth, it was bound to be the case in a period during which there was so much discussion about the base communities, another of liberation theology's great themes should be ecclesiology.[19] One of the great theological debates in Latin America is about the new church forms. Those who defend a traditional view of the Church regard it as necessary that ecclesiatical institutions should maintain their hierarchical structure—and thus, their power. For those who support the church forms arising from the people, the priority is the communion of the people of God. Without denying the importance of organic church structure, liberation theology comes down on the side of a church which becomes the people and is manifested as communion.[20]

Seventh, in relation to the economic challenges mentioned earlier thinking has been developing about the relationship between economics and theology. This is one of the most interesting aspects of liberation theology, as it attempts to discern the fetishistic and idolatrous tendencies in current policital and neo-classical economics. This culminates in the affirmation of faith in the liberating God of Jesus Christ who is the God of life.[21] In countries where, as we said earlier, workers' lives are sacrificed to the greed of dominant economic interests, these statements have a very strong impact on community members.

Eighth, the need for Christians to take part in political life and movements has led to reflection on Christian political ethics, based on experience. This reflection has an important eschatological orientation, emphasising the social side of the Kingdom of God as an essential part of the Gospel.[22]

We cannot end this brief essay without mentioning one very important factor. This is that theology has moved home. Now it is not the Church allied to the established power (Christendom), or the Church legitimising its own economic power and hegemony in the historical process. Liberation theologians do their work at home with the people, the poor with them, through them and for them. It therefore comes as no surprise if theologians—men and women—sometimes experience suffering, as the poor do. United with them in church life, they cannot escape their fate in confronting the powerful of this world. This is both a sign of communion and also a witness (*martyria*) which gives substance and credibility to Latin American liberation theology. It grows out of the life of the people's Christian communities and turns back to them in a self-offering to God.

Translated by Dinah Livingstone

Notes

1. Especially Gustavo Gutiérrez and Leonardo Boff. A period of silence was imposed on the latter between May 1985 and April 1986.

2. See the two *Instructions* on liberation theology published by the Holy See in September 1984 and March 1986.

3. For example in Brazil in 1978, a worker received a wage equivalent to $US162 per month, whereas by the end of 1987 the value of the minimum wage was $US40.

4. It is worth mentioning the debate that took place between various Brazilian theologians and social scientists: Fr. Clodovis Boff, Fr. Betto, Pedro Ribeiro de Oliveira, Herbert de Sousa, Luiz Eduardo Wanderley etc. See *Tempo e Presença*, (Rio de Janeiro CEDI, August 1986 and March 1987).

5. Havanna, 1986. Also in Portuguese: *Fidel e a Religião* (Rio de Janerio 1986).

6. Report given by the Latin American Region to the Second General Assembly of the Ecumenical Association of Third World Theologians (EATWOT) in Oactepec, Mexico, December.

7. See Julio de Santa Ana *Ecumenismo* (Madrid 1987).

8. This idea prevailed for a while among European and North American theologians, including those who sympathised with liberation theology. See Georges Casalis *Les Idées Justes ne tombent pas du Ciel* (Paris 1978).

9. Collection containing more than twenty published volumes of the 54 planned (Madrid & Buenos Aires)

10. See the biblical collection being published in Brazil by the combined efforts of three publishers: Vozes, Sinodal and Imprensa Metodista. See also the collection published in Buenos Aires by La Aurora.

11. See Gustavo Gutiérrez *Beber en su propio pozo* (Lima 1983).

12. For CEHILA's publications consult its permanent secretariat: Rue Martiniano de Carvalho 114, Bela Vista, 01321 São Paulo, S,P., Brazil.

13. Most of these theologians are laywomen, which increases the interest of their contributions.

14. *Jesucristo Libertador* (Petropolis 1972).

15. *Cristologśa desde América Latina* (Bilbao 1977).

16. *El Hombre de Hoy frente a Jesús de Nazaret*, 3 vols. (Madrid 1982).

17. *O Significado político da Morte de Jesus* (Petropolis 1981).

18. *El Proyect de Jesús* (Lima 1980).

19. See Leonardo Boff *Igreja, Carisma e Poder* (Petropolis 1981); Pablo Richard *Muerte de las Cristiandades y Nacimiento de la Iglesia* (San Josè, Costa Rica 1982); Ronaldo Muñoz *Nueva Conciencia de la Iglesia en América Latina* (Santiago, Chile).

20. See especially Leonardo Boff *E a Igreja se fez Povo* (Petropolis 1986).

21. See various authors *La Lucha de los Dioses* (San José, Costa Rica 1980).; Franz Hinkelammert *Democracia y Totalitarismo* (San José, Costa Rica 1987).

22. José Miguez Bonino *Toward a Christian Political Ethics* (New York 1985).

James Cone

Theologies of Liberation Among US Racial-Ethnic Minorities

THERE ARE four major groups of racial-ethnic minorities in the United States who are members of the Ecumenical Association of Third World Theologians (EATWOT): Native-Americans, African-Americans, Hispanic-Americans, and Asian-Americans. Each of these groups has complex and different histories and cultures which have influenced the origin and the development of their theological discourse. Theology is always made when people seek to understand the ultimate meaning of their existence in relation to their neighbours and their God. Who are we? Why were we created? What is our purpose in the world? *How* a people answers these questions, and the *sources* from which they derive the answers, define the nature of their theological discourse.

To be oppressed means that a people's answers to questions about their identity have been imposed upon them. In the United States, racial-ethnic minorities live in a society whose religio-cultural and socio-political values have been defined by an ideology of white supremacy. The English Puritans who landed at Plymouth Rock in 1620 believed that they were God's chosen people, the new Israel, elected by God to civilise and Christianise the 'New World'. Their idea of Christianity emphasised not only the Calvinist theme of the absolute sovereignty of God but also a similar rule of the white Anglo-Saxon race over others. 'The white race [was] the normal or typical

Note: I am especially grateful to Father Virgilio Elizondo for his contribution to this essay. He was particularly helpful in the section on Hispanic-Americans, writing much of it himself.

race', they contended. 'The Anglo-Saxon and Anglo-American,' wrote the highly-regarded Church historian Philip Schaff, 'of all modern races, possess the strongest national character and the one best fitted for universal dominion.'[1]

The dominant expression of Christianity in the United States has been primarily Protestant. However, the Catholic Church, though a minority denomination and often itself persecuted, supported the white Protestant ruling class in their justification of the right of whites to exterminate, enslave, and segregate non-Europeans. Protestants and Catholics not only provide religious justification for the government's exploitation of minorities, they also oppressed them within their own communions. The indigenous people, blacks, hispanics, and asians, were defined as the 'other' who either had to be converted to the 'white Christian way of life' by willingly accepting their inferior status—or they did not deserve to exist. 'A good Indian is a dead Indian' was the expression of this value in the popular mind of white America in relation to the original people of the continent. Similar dehumanising characterisations were made in regard to minorities from Africa, Latin America, and Asia. To be 'coloured' in the United States meant to be only partly human—'three-fifth' was the portion set for African slaves by the Founding Fathers in the Constitution of 1787.

As long as racial-ethnics accepted their assigned places in society as defined by the dominant white race, they were often allowed to exist. Many minorities, however, resisted white definition of their humanity and fiercely asserted their own right to define the terms of their existence. The history of America is also the history of their resistance. It is a history from the *underside* of the American story—largely invisible to others who do not share or identify with its legacy.

To understand the rise of liberation theology among racial-ethnic minorities in the United States, it is necessary to know something of the history of their struggle to be recognised as first class citizens in a land defined for whites only. Our liberation theologies have not been borrowed from Latin America, Africa, or Asia, even though we have been greatly stimulated by our brothers and sisters of the Third World and have learned much from them. Our thinking about God, however, has been initiated by and created out of our different cultural histories and our continuing struggles for freedom in the United States. Because sheer physical and mental survival has been the dominant concern of most of our people, civil rights has been the primary focus of our liberation struggles rather than the search for global solidarity with our brothers and sisters in the Third World.

Recently, however, a great change has come over many of us. We now recognise, as never before in our history, that our liberation in the US is inseperably linked with the freedom of the poor in the Third World. EATWOT has played an important role in this regard. But much more important has been our own practice and reflection which revealed the great limitation of our fight for civil rights. We have discovered that our oppression is deeply rooted in the US political economy and its global manifestations. The same white ruling class that oppresses US minorities also stretches its capitalist arms into many lands and cultures throughout Asia, Africa, and Latin America and exploits the masses of the people for its own material profit. On the basis of our own experience of struggle, many of us discovered that Third World liberation movements were not separate from our own. On the contrary, all movements of freedom among the poor, here and abroad, are inseparably bound together. Liberation movements in South Africa, Korea, and Central America have made a strong impact upon our fight for justice in the United States. Their struggle and ours are one: As Martin Luther King, Jr, put it:

We are caught up in an inescapable network of mutality, tied to a single garment of destiny. What affects one directly, affects all indirectly. As long as there is poverty in this world, no [one] can be totally rich. . . . As long as diseases are rampant and millions of people cannot expect to live more than twenty or thirty years, no [one] can be totally healthy. . . . Strangely enough, I can never be what I ought to be until you are what you ought to be. You can never be what you ought to be until I am what I ought to be.[2]

Although US minorities realise that our struggles for freedom are linked with Third World liberation movements, this universal note does not replace the need for us to begin our own theological reflections, using our particular histories and cultures as the primary sources for our thinking. Some of our Third World brothers and sisters have not always appreciated this point and have often encouraged us to repeat their theological formulations rather than develop our own. Others have even suggested that our theological sensibilities are so controlled by the First World that we do not have any distinct contribution to make that is different from the progressive theologies of the United States and Europe. They even questioned whether we should be participants in EATWOT.

If liberation theologies among US minorities are to be correctly understood, it is necessary to know something about the various histories and cultures that give birth to them. They cannot be correctly interpreted by using the historical and theological categories of white oppressors. Neither can they be placed in one general theological framework, as if they share the same cultural history and perspective on God. As the liberation theologies in Latin America, Africa, and Asia are different, so are the theological reflections among minorities in the US. We are not only different; *our differences sometimes clash*. Racial-ethnics in the US live in separate communities and our mutual white oppressors are often quite successful in dividing us from each other, thereby creating animosities between our communities. Many of us, however, are determined to overcome the barriers that separate us so that we can make common cause in our struggle for freedom. But we cannot achieve genuine solidarity with each other unless we show mutual respect and appreciation for the uniqueness of each other's cultural history.

1. NATIVE AMERICANS

The original people of the North American continent have been called 'Indians', 'First Americans', 'Indigenous people', and 'Native Americans'. Like many people whom the white Europeans encountered, they were nearly exterminated, and those who manage to survive have been pushed off their land and placed on reservations. Today they are the most oppressed and ignored people of all US minorities. Native Americans are currently engaged in legal battles, trying to retain or regain their land from greedy capitalists so as to preserve their cultures and histories.

In the popular mind of America and in the discourse on its history and politics, the Native people of this land are often invisible. They are defined by their absence from the dominant discourse about the meaning of American life and culture. Unfortunately, Native Americans are also often absent from the discourse of other US minorities who are challenging the dominant white understanding of America. But their absence in our discourse is itself a 'striking presence'.[3]

Recently, prominent voices have begun to emerge from the Native American community. One of the most articulate and radical thinkers among them is Vine Deloria, Jr, an EATWOT member and the author of *Custer Died for Your Sins* (1969), *We Talk, You Listen* (1970), and *God is Red* (1973). He is a Sioux Indian, a lawyer and theologian who has been deeply engaged in defending the rights of his people in the legal courts, universities and theological seminaries, and other public gatherings.

Deloria is especially critical of the western orientation of Christianity and the theologies which emerged out of it. Even liberation theologians do not escape his critique. He contends that if we are seeking genuine liberation, then we must begin to question the way we think, even about liberation, so that we can move beyond our western world-view. Speaking to a workshop on liberation theology, sponsored by the Theology in the Americas (TIA) in New York (June 1978), Deloria shocked his audience of mostly white, liberation-conscious Americans when he said:

> Now, let's not kid ourselves. If we all believe in liberation theology completely, I would be the only one in this room. Right? The rest of you, having helped us liberate North America, would be comfortably entrenched in Europe. So let's not get carried away with sincerity and fanaticism about this topic.[4]

His concern was to challenge his audience to move their thinking about the US society and the world beyond Christianity or Marxism by questioning the western thought patterns from which both were derived. He encouraged them to consider the 'Indian way' which was more holistic, spiritual and earth-centred.

In another essay, Deloria contended that even liberation theology 'does not seek to destroy the roots of oppression, but merely changes the manner in which oppression manifests itself'. The problem, according to Deloria, is the way white men think about the world which inevitably leads to their violation of the earth and humanity. What is needed is 'the destruction of the whole complex of Western theories of knowledge and the construction of new and more comprehensive synthesis of human knowledge and experience. . . . Then we are speaking truly of liberation. For it is the manner in which people conceive reality that motivates them to behave in certain ways.' In a provocative illustration, he wrote: 'The white man . . . has ideas: Indians have visions. Ideas have a single dimension. . . . The vision, on the other hand, presents a whole picture of experience and has a central meaning that stands on its own feet as an independent revelation.'[5]

2. AFRICAN-AMERICANS

No people have provided a greater challenge to the public meaning of the United States as 'the land of the free and the home of the brave' than its citizens of African descent. Unlike Europeans who came freely to the Americas, Africans came against their will on slave ships and were sold as *property*. It is difficult for those who do not have a slave legacy to know what it means for a people to be defined as property. To be property meant that you and your descendants were not fully human beings. Your worth, therefore, was defined by the price which interested bidders were willing to pay in a slave market. Family ties, of course, could be disregarded, along with other aspects of human dignity that most people took for granted in a civilised society.

African presence in North America began in 1619, one year before the English Pilgrims landed at Plymouth Rock. Referring to our prior, involuntary presence and subsequent servitude, Malcolm X often reminded white Americans that 'we are Africans who happen to be in America. . . . We didn't land on Plymouth Rock. It landed on us.'[6] After two hundred and forty-four years of legal slavery, it was abolished in 1863. But the oppression of blacks continued in another form that was called *segregation*—the American version of *Apartheid*. Some people said that segregation was worse than slavery, because the newly freed slaves were not only property-less; their livelihood was still dependent upon their former slave masters. Martin Luther King, Jr, often referred to segregation as 'another form of slavery dressed up in certain niceties of complexity'.

Black resistance began during slavery, and it has continued to the present day. The idea that blacks were passive and accepted freely their oppression is a myth promoted by whites to justify their evil deeds. African resistance to slavery took many forms. It was collective and individual, violent and non-violent, religious and secular in its orientation.

Like other US minorities, the religion of blacks has been important in empowering them in their struggle for survival and liberation. Black religion has been defined by two main elements: its African heritage and its encounter with the Christianity of white missionaries. With these two elements, blacks developed a distinctive religion that is neither exclusively Christian (when 'Christianity' is defined by European specifications) nor primarily African (when 'African' is defined by African Traditional Religions). Black religion was created primarily out of black people's struggle to liberate themselves from the oppression of whites.

The uniqueness of black religion led to the development of independent religious institutions, which have been and still are primarily Christian and mostly Protestant. The oldest black independent churches were founded in the late eighteenth century, and they played significant roles in the abolitionist and insurrectionist movements in the nineteenth century. Gabriel Prosser, Denmark Vesey, and Nat Turner were prominent revolutionaries who used religion in their slave revolts.

Martin Luther King, Jr, and Malcolm X are twentieth century examples of blacks who used religion in their fight for freedom. Martin King was a Christian minister, and Malcolm was a Muslim minister. King was an integrationist and advocate of non-violence. Malcolm was a separatist and a promoter of self-defence. King spoke eloquently about the possibility of the 'American dream'; but Malcolm did not let us forget the reality of the

'American nightmare'. These two black freedom-fighters and freedom-sayers dominated the consciousness of the African-American freedom struggle during the fifties and sixties.

Black theology was created during the sixties as black Christian activists—mostly ministers—attempted to reconcile Martin King's idea of love and non-violence with Malcolm X's emphasis on blackness and self-defence. 'Black' in black theology represents our allegiance to Malcolm X, and 'theology' in the phrase designates our commitment to Martin King. Black theology's focus on the central theme of *liberation* represents our commitment to both Martin and Malcolm, martyrs who freely gave their lives for the freedom of our people. Together Martin and Malcolm remind us that there can be no freedom for black people unless it is derived from the particularity of our cultural history (Malcolm) and which also moves beyond itself to embrace the freedom of all people (Martin).

Albert B. Cleage, a strong advocate of Black Power and the pastor of the Shrine of the Black Madonna in Detroit, Michigan, did much to initiate the discussion on black theology with the publication of his highly controversial book entitled, *The Black Messiah* (1968). A few months later, James Cone's *Black Theology and Black Power* (1969) appeared. It was followed by his *A Black Theology of Liberation* (1970). Other black theologians and preachers joined Cleage and Cone, challenging them to move closer to the thinking of either Martin King or Malcolm X. Prominent publications included J. Deotis Robert's *Liberation and Reconciliation: A Black Theology* (1971), Major J. Jones, *Black Awareness: A Theology of Hope* (1971), and Gayraud S. Wilmore's *Black Religion and Black Radicalism* (1972).

More recently, black theologians have begun to address the issues of Marxism and feminism. EATWOT has been influential for the former, and white feminists have influenced the latter. Cornel West has emerged as the most creative and influential thinker on Marxism among black theologians. His book, *Prophesy Deliverance!* (1982), is his most important text on the subject. Influential black women theologians include Delores Williams, Kelly Brown, Jackie Grant, and Katie Cannon.

3. HISPANIC-AMERICANS

Although Hispanic-Americans have always been a part of the present day United States, they have never been recognised or treated as ordinary citizens. They became part of the US way of conquest and not through migration. Generally speaking, Hispanics can be characterised as a people who have been *twice conquered, twice colonised,* and *twice 'mestisised'.* The first process started with the arrival of the first European illegal immigrant, Christopher Columbus in 1492. The second began in the 1830s when the US confiscated fifty per cent of Mexico (from California to Texas) and all of Puerto Rico in 1897. Thus the Mexicans and the Puerto Ricans discovered themselves to be foreigners in their own land.

Because of the initial contacts which gave birth to what today we call Hispanic-Americans, these two groups—Mexicans and Puerto Ricans—have never had a sense of migration but rather of having been a colonised people who, *regardless of the passage of time,* want their original traditions, language, and life-styles to *survive* and *flourish* in the United States.

During this colonial existence, Hispanics have been exploited economically, denied educational opportunities, effectively distanced from participation in the political system, portrayed as irresponsible and inferior by all the media of communication, kept out of the structures of society and ignored by their church (mainly Catholic). Yet, in spite of the multiple obstacles and threats against their collective existence as Hispanics, they have not only survived but today are the fastest growing minority group in the US.

The struggle for justice has always been a part of the life of Hispanics; however—as with blacks—it was intensified following their experience in World War II. War veterans discovered that the principles of freedom and democracy which they fought for abroad were denied them upon their return home to the United States. The fight was on. Ya Basta (That's enough) became the battle cry as Hispanic-Americans fought for justice and equality in their own native land. Movements started from the *barrios* to the universities, from farm-workers to government employees, from political parties to church institutions. No area of American life was left unchallenged.

Hispanic religion has had an enormous impact upon their liberation struggle. Like black religion, it can be defined by two elements: its native American heritage and its encounter with white missionaries. However, it differs in that the indigenous religions of their native ancestors were different from African religious traditions and white missionaries were marked by all the characteristics of the Iberian Catholicism of that period which was quite different from the Catholicism or Protestantism of the rest of Europe.

The Hispanic religion of the masses is a direct contact and celebration of God's presence without the intermediary of the institution or the sacraments of the Church. Generally speaking, the people tolerate the clergy but do not consider them to be a part of their ordinary religious expression. The clergy person appears a *distant other* and not as one of the people. Hence the clergy appear more as *icons* than as *ministers.* This is undoubtedly due to the fact that—unlike black Protestant churches—Hispanics, who are mostly

Catholics, do not serve as pastors. Even though thirty per cent of all US Catholics are Hispanics, less than two per cent of the total clergy are native born Hispanics. They have no churches, seminaries, colleges, or church institutions that they can truly call their own. The only exception is the Mexican American Cultural Center (MACC) in San Antonio, Texas. Thus a Hispanic theology of liberation is in its early stages of development.

One of the most influential and articulate interpreters of liberation theology among Hispanics is Father Virgilio Elizondo, founder and president of MACC, EATWOT member, and author of the influential text, *Galilean Journey: The Mexican-American Promise* (1983). This text is both historical and theological, focusing on the story of Mexican-Americans in North America and their significance in relation to the Gospel story of Jesus, the Galilean. Andres Guerrero's *A Chicano Theology* (1986) is another important theological text that has emerged out of the Hispanic community. Prominent Protestant theologians include Justo L. Gonzalez—a Cuban and an outstanding historian; and Jorge Lara-Braud, a Mexican-American professor of theology. Ada Maria Isasi-Diaz, a Cuban, is making a significant contribution in the area of feminist theology. Important writings by Hispanic-Americans are found in *Apuntes*, a journal published quarterly by the Mexican American Program at Perkins School of Theology in Dallas, Texas.

4. ASIAN-AMERICANS

Asian presence in the US began in the nineteenth century and has continued to the present day. Like other minorities, they have experienced severe discrimination and other forms of oppression. The colourful phrases 'yellow peril' and 'red scare' symbolise white America's attitude towards Asians. From 1850 to 1950, successive waves of Chinese, Japanese, Filipinos, Koreans, and Pacific Islanders immigrated to the US and were often viewed as a peril that must be driven back or kept in place. The 'red scare' referred to the People's Republic of China. However, the most blatant expression of America's unjust treatment of Asians was the internment of 110,000 Japanese Americans during World War II without due process of law.

Asian-Americans often have the image of the model minority. In great contrast with Indians, Hispanics and Blacks, they have demonstrated their ability to overcome great obstacles, competing on a par with white Americans and in some instances proving themselves more successful. More recently, however, some Asians began to question their so-called 'success' in America. Roy I. Sano, a Japanese theologian and now a United Methodist Bishop, reflecting on his personal experience of political powerlessness, put it this way: 'While the acculturation and assimilation of Asian Americans . . . may have produced conspicuous examples of people living *above* that "poverty line", reflections on our [experience in this society] clearly demonstrated how much we [have] operated *below* the "power line".'[7] This also led him to suggest that the Old Testament story of *Esther* rather than *Ruth* is the most appropriate model for the Asian experience in America. 'The story of Ruth is at best a dream, if not a delusion.' (251) Esther, 'who had obtained entrance into an alien society', recovered her 'ethnic identity and reversed the decree against her people'.[8] Sano also urges a similar preference for apocalypticism over prophecy, because the former represents a period when Israel's nationhood was lost, forcing the people to search for meaning as their lives were controlled by foreign powers.

Other prominent Asian-Americans theologians include Wesley Woo and Rita Brock, a feminist. The most important text is *The Theologians of Asian Americans and Pacific Peoples: A Reader*, compiled by Roy Sano and published by the Asian Centre for Theology and Strategies (1976).

5. A COMMON THEME

While there are different historical experiences of racial-ethnic minorities, thereby creating different theological emphases, there is none-the-less a common theme among them. It is found in the search for *cultural identity* in a society defined by white supremacy. To be 'coloured' in white America creates a 'hyphenated-existence', a 'double consciousness'. The classic statement of this paradox for African-Americans was written by W. E. B. DuBois in 1903:

> It is a peculiar sensation, this double consciousness, this sense of always looking at one's self through the eyes of others, of measuring one's soul by the tape of a world that looks on in amused contempt and pity. One ever feels this two-ness—an American, a Negro; two souls, two thoughts, two unreconciled strivings; two warring ideals in one dark body, whose dogged strength alone keeps it from being torn asunder.[9]

In their mutual search for identity, racial-ethnics have only begun to develop theological reflections out of a praxis for justice which we share in common. Small beginnings have taken place in grass-roots communities and also in TIA and in EATWOT. But there is much theological work still to be done in our communities before a meaningful coalition can be achieved. Presidential candidate Jesse Jackson's 'Rainbow Coalition' and the election of

Harold Washington as Mayor of Chicago are the most promising examples of minorities working together in politics. Let us hope that a solidarity in liberation movements among poor minorities will serve as the first step toward a coalition in theology.

Notes

1. Martin E. Marty *Righteous Empire: The Protestant Experience in America* (New York 1970) pp. 14,17.
2. Martin L. King, Jr, 'The American Dream' in *A Testament of Hope: The Essential Writings of Martin Luther King, Jr*, ed. James Washington (San Francisco 1986) 210.
3. I first heard this phrase in a conversation with Father Virgilio Elizondo.
4. V. Deloria, Jr 'A Native American Perspective on Liberation Theology' in *Is Liberation Theology for North America?: The Response of First World Churches* (pamphlet published by Theology in the Americas, New York) p. 12.
5. V. Deloria, Jr 'A Native American Perspective on Liberation' in *Mission Trends No. 4: Liberation Theologies in North America and Europe*, ed. G. Anderson & T. Stransky (New York 1979), pp. 262, 269, 270, 268.
6. Quoted in Helen Dubar, 'The Muslims and Black Nationalism', *Post Daily Magazine*, 10 April 1964.
7. Roy I. Sano 'Transforming Suffering' in *Changing Contexts of our Faith*, ed. Letty Russell (Philadelphia 1985) p. 70.
8. Roy I. Sano, 'Ethnic Liberation Theology: Neo-Orthodoxy Reshaped or Replaced?' in *Mission Trends No. 4* p. 251.
9. W. E. B. DuBois *The Souls of Black Folk* (Greenwich, Conn. 1961) pp. 16–17.

PART III

'I Bless you Father for Revealing these Things to Little Children'

Justin Ukpong

Theological Literature from Africa

AFRICA THEOLOGIANS distinguish between *Inculturation theology, Feminist theology, Black theology* and *Liberation theology*. Inculturation theology, also called *African theology* or *African Christian theology*, is a creative encounter between African thought system and European Christian thought system. Feminist theology addresses the issue of sexism; Black theology the issue of racism in South Africa; and Liberation theology addresses oppressive economic and political (civil and ecclesiastical) structures. Liberation theology is taken here in the narrow sense; in the wide sense, it includes all the other theologies except inculturation theology.[1]

In this article, I shall discuss selected authors in the different areas indicated here.

1. INCULTURATION THEOLOGY

Inculturation theology has its background and origin in the attempt of the early missionaries to interpret the Christian message in terms of African concepts.[2] It seeks to integrate Christianity with African life and thought.

The appearance in 1946 of Placide Tempels' *La Philosophie bantoue* (Paris tr. *Bantu Philosophy* 1959) marked the beginning of the modern age of African theological literature. This was Tempels hand-maid to a Christian theology that would be African. Convinced that Africans had a system of thought different from the Westerners', Tempels worked out an African

67

ontology based on the concept of 'vital force' in Bantu thought. This refers to the participation of all beings, visible and invisible, in one process of interaction. He applied this ontology in his pastoral reflections. In 1949 he published *La Christianisation des Philosophies Paiennes*. Tempels laid the foundations for today's African Philosophy and African theology.

In 1955, a group of African and Haitian priests studying in Rome met to discuss the problem of relating the Christian message to the life and thought of their people. The term 'African Theology' was first used by M. Hebga at this discussion[3] from which emanated a collection of essays published in 1956 with the title *Des Prêtres Noirs S'interrogent* (*Paris: CERF*).

Vincent Mulago is a professor of theology at the Catholic Theological Faculty, Kinshasa. Writing in the tradition established by Tempels, he sees African communal meals as a suitable model for explaining the Eucharist (see his article in *Des Prêtres Noirs* mentioned above). In his *Un Visage Africain du Christianisme* (Paris 1965) he modifies Tempels' concept of 'vital force' with 'vital union' or 'vital participation'.

Tshishiku Tshibangu, a Catholic Bishop and Rector of the National University of Zaire brings a sociological perspective to African theology. In his *Théologie Positive et Théologie Spéculative Position Traditionelle et Nouvelle Problématique* (Paris 1965), he studies the history of theological methodology pointing out new insights for African theology. In another book, *La Théologie Comme Science au xxème Siècle* (Zaire 1980) he shows how theology should be related to the people and their society.

Ngindu Mushete, is a professor of Fundamental theology at the Catholic Theological Faculty, Kinshasa, Zaire and also editor of *African Theology Bulletin*. He advocates an approach in African Theology that involves the exposure of the totality of African life and thought to the Christian message. His publications include *La Problème de la Connaissance Religiouse d'après L. Laberthonnière* (Kinshasa 1977); 'Courantes Actuels De La Théologie En Afrique' (*Bulletin of African Theology* 6 (1984) 247–252); 'The Notion of Truth in African Theology' (*CONCILIUM* 192 (1987) 53–63).

Aylward Shorter W. F., a missionary priest and an anthropologist, is a professor of theology at the Catholic Higher Institute of Eastern Africa (CHIEA), Nairobi. He emphasises the need to develop theology 'from below', and to start with the pastoral realities and the experience of the faith community. He uses his anthropological training to provide insights into the deeper values of African culture. His publications include *African Christian Theology: Adaptation or Incarnation?* (London 1975); *African Christian Spirituality* (London 1975); *African Christian Spirituality* (London 1978).

Charles Nyamiti, a Tanzanian and professor of theology at CHIEA advocates the use of African conceptual categories to explain Christian doctrine. His publications include *The Way to Christian Theology for Africa* (Eldoret, Kenya 1978); *African Tradition and the Christian God* (Eldoret 1977); *Christ the Ancestor* (Harare 1984).

John S. Mbiti, a theology professor from Kenya, was formerly the director of the World Council of Churches' Ecumenical Institute at Bossey near Geneva. He rejects Tempels' notion of 'vital force' and employs a phenomenological approach to African theology. His publications include, *Concepts of God in Africa* (London 1970); *African Religions and Philosophy* (London 1969); *New Testament Eschatology in An African Background* (London 1970).

E. B. Idowu formerly a professor of Religion at Ibadan University, Nigeria and now retired Nigerian Methodist Church Primate, rejects, like Mbiti, Tempels' concept of 'vital force' and uses a phenomenological approach to African theology. He calls for African theology that will respond to the African's social, political spiritual and emotional needs. His works include *Towards an Indigenous Church* (Oxford 1965); *Olodumare: God in Yoruba Belief* (London 1962); *Job: A Meditation on Suffering* (Ibadan 1976).

Barthelemy Adoukonou, an anthropologist and theologian from Benin Republic, applies the structuralism of Levi-Strauss and the hermeneutics of Paul Ricoeur in his theological approach. He seeks, through this method, to bring about a creative encounter between African values and the Christian faith. His major publication is *Jalons pour une théologie africaine* (Paris 1979, in two volumes).

Douglas Makhathini teaches at the Lutheran Theological College, Mapumulo, Zululand, South Africa. He seeks to express biblical reflections in African categories; and in his essay, 'Black Theology', he shows the relevance of inculturation theology even in the context of racial discrimination and the deprecation of African culture (see H. J. Beckan ed. *Relevant Theology for Africa* Durban 1973).

Patrick Kalilombe, a Catholic Bishop from Malawi, currently teaches at the Selly Oaks College, Birmingham. For him, African theology must be a grass roots theology which means not theologising *about* or *for* the people, but theologising *with* the people. His publications include *From Outstation to Small Christian Community* (Eldoret, Kenya 1984); 'Doing Theology at the Grassroots: A Challenge for professional Theologians' (*AFER* 27 (1985) 148–161 and 225–237.

Emefie Ikenga Metuh, a Catholic priest and professor of Religion at the University of Jos, Nigeria, emphasises that African religious thought must be interpreted with the African and not with the Western conceptual frame of reference. Among his publications are *God and Man in African Religion* (London 1981); *African Religions in Western Conceptual Schemes: The Problem of Interpretation* (Ibadan 1985).

Gwuriyai H. Muzorewa of the United Methodist Church teaches at the United Theological College in Harare, Zimbabwe. For him, African epistemology must govern the articulation of African theology; and the African Church must respond positively to political, economic, social and religious issues. His major publication is *The Origins and Development of African Theology* (Orbis 1985).

Kwesi Dickson. Unlike most of the authors discussed above, Dickson and the others we shall discuss below bring a specifically biblical orientation to African theology. A professor of religion at the University of Ghana, Dickson emphasises biblical studies from African perspectives at the starting point for African theology. His publications include the series *The History and Religion of Israel* (London 1968–); *Theology in Africa* (Mary Knoll 1984).

John S. Pobee, a Ghanaian and formerly a professor at the University of Ghana, is currently associate director of the World Council of Churches' Programme on Theological Education, Geneva. His writings cover both inculturation and liberation issues. He insists on the recognition of certain non-negotiable elements in Christianity in the process of inculturation and, like Dickson, advocates a re-reading of the bible from the African perspective. Among his numerous publications are *Toward an African Theology* (Nashville 1979); *Who are the Poor?* (Geneva 1987).

Daniel N. Wambutda, an Old Testament scholar and professor of Religion at the University of Jos, Nigeria, sees the hermeneutical circle approach as most suitable for contextualising the biblical message. His publications include, 'Hermeneutics and the search for Theologia Africana' (*Africa Theological Journal* (1980, 29–39); 'Savannah Theology—A Biblical Reconsideration of the Concept of Salvation in the African Context' (*Bulletin of African Theology* 3(1981) 137–154).

Christ U. Manus, a New Testament scholar at Obafemi Awolowo University Ife, Nigeria, seeks to understand the biblical message in the context of African religious experience and cultural values. His publications include 'Gal. 3:28—Study on Paul's Attitude Towards Christianity: Its Relevance for Contemporary Nigeria' (*Ife Journal of Religion* (1982) 18–26); 'The Areopagus Speech (Acts 17:16–34): A Study of Luke's Approach to Evangelism and Its Significance in the African Context' (*Africa Theological Journal* 14(1985)3–18).

F. Eboussi Boulaga, a Cameroonian and professor of Philosophy at the National University of the Ivory Coast, is a class apart from the other theologians so far considered in terms of his approach and methodology. While the others take cultural values or the biblical text as their starting point, the point of departure for Boulaga is a critique of missionary Christianity in Africa; and while the methodology of the others may be described as propositional, his is narrative. In his major work *Christianity Without Fetishes: An African Critique and Recapture of Christianity* (Orbis 1984) he sees inculturation as involving more the question of power-sharing than cosmetic adaptation.

2. FEMINIST THEOLOGY

Women liberation struggles have been taking place in different forms in Africa over the years. An example is the women's revolt against colonial oppressive measures in Aba, Nigeria in 1929. However, it is only recently that these struggles have become a theological issue. Feminist theology seeks to clarify the identity of women as equal partners with men in the human community. The point of departure is the biblical story of creation (Gen. 1:26–26) whereby God made man and woman in his own image.

Mercy Amba Oduyeye, formerly lecturer at the University of Ibadan, Nigeria, and currently deputy general secretary of the World Council of Churches, Geneva, has written on feminist and inculturation issues. She challenges Third World theologians to see the women issue as a priority, and calls for a theological redefinition of the concepts of headship, authority and power in the light of the gospels. She is the author of 'The Roots of African Christian Feminism' (*Variations in African Theology*, ed. John S. Pobee and Carl F. Hallencreutz. Nairobi 1986 pp. 33–47), *Hearing and Knowing: Theological Reflections on Christianity in Africa* (Orbis 1986).

Teresa Okure, SHCJ, a New Testament scholar at the Catholic Institute of West Africa, Port Harcourt, Nigeria, and the executive secretary of the Ecumenical Association of Third World theologians calls for a rehabilitation of the image of the woman in Church and society from a biblical perspective. She sees the continued exclusion of women from participation in certain Christian ministeries as arising from cultural bias. Her publications include 'Biblical Perspectives on Women: Eve the Mother of the Living (Gen. 3:20)' (*Voices from the Third World* 8(1985)17–24); 'Justice and Compassion: A Biblical Perspective' (*Source* 16(1987)5–18).

Rosemary Edet, HHCJ, another Nigerian religious and theologian teaching at the University of Calabar, Nigeria, has written on women and inculturation issues. She urges that women be moved from the periphery to the centre of the Church's life and activity. Her publications include, *From Nature to Divine: An Introduction to the Study of Religions* (co-author)

(Rome 1984); 'Women in Church Life' (EATWOT Conference Paper, Mexico 1986).

Bette J. Ekeya, a Kenyan and lecturer at the University of Nairobi, has emphasised the involvement of women at the grassroots in the elaboration of theology. She sees the image of the victorious Christ as most relevant in evolving an African Christology from women's perspective. She is author of 'Christ in the Various Experience in which Women Do Theology' (EATWOT Conference paper, Mexico 1986).

Sister Justine Kahungu Mbwiti from Zaire sees Jesus as the liberator of women who went contrary to the norms of his society in respect of women and thus gave a new perspective for understanding the role of women in church and society. She is author of 'La Femme Das L'Eglise' (*EATWOT Commission on Theology From Third World Women's Perspective: General Report*. Yaounde 1986).

Rose Zoe-Obianga, is a Cameroonian and the coordinator, for Africa, of the Commission on theology from Third World Women's Perspective. In her paper, 'The Role of Women in present Day Africa' (*African Theology En Route*, ed. Kofi Appiah-Kusi and Sergio Torres, Orbis, 1979 pp. 145–149), she cautions that it is the Church that loses by excluding women from its centre of life and action.

3. SOUTH AFRICAN BLACK THEOLOGY

South African Black theology has its background and context in the protracted struggle, since the seventeenth century, of native South Africans against racism, colonialism and institutionalised exploitation enforced upon them by their European colonisers. Out of this struggle eventually emerged, in the twentieth century, the philosophy of Black consciousness and Black theology.

The Challenge of Black Theology in South Africa, ed. Basil Moore (Atlanta 1974). This collection of articles is one of the earliest publications on Black Theology.

Steve Biko, an ardent promoter of the Black consciousness movement and of Black theology, was arrested in 1977 and tortured, and eventually died. He was instrumental to the founding of the South African Students Organisation in 1969. He is author of 'Black consciousness and the Quest for a true Humanity' in *The Challenge of Black Theology in South Africa*.

Desmond Tutu, the Anglican Archbishop of Cape Town and the 1984 Nobel Peace Prize winner sees the apartheid regime in South Africa as the most savage since that of Nazi Germany. He is the author of 'Black Theology' (*Frontier* 17(1974)73–76); 'Black Theology/African Theology: Soul Mates or Antagonists?' (*Journal of Religious Thought* 33(1975)25–33); 'The Theology of Liberation in Africa' (*African Theology En route*).

Allan Boesak is Chaplain at the University of Western Cape and President of the World Alliance of Reformed Churches. He sees God and Jesus in the biblical context of liberation, and affirms Christ as the 'Black Messiah'. His most important publication is *Farewell to Innocence: A Socio-Ethical Study on Black Theology and Power* (Orbis 1977).

Manas Buthelezi rejects inculturation theology in South Africa and finds only Black Theology relevant. He insists on the need to grapple with social and essential issues of the society. He has published, 'An African Theology or Black Theology?' (*The Challenge of Black Theology* pp. 29–35); 'Toward Indigenous Theology in South Africa' (*The Emergent Gospel*, ed. Sergio Torres and Virginia Fabella; Orbis pp. 56–75).

Simon Maimela, a professor at the University of Pretoria in South Africa, sees Black theology as an attempt to show that God has authorised Black existence as a legitimate form of human existence. In his assessment, 'white' theology presents man as a dangerous monster. He is author of, 'Black Power and Black Theology in Southern Africa' (*Scripture* 12(1984)40–53); 'Man in "white" Theology' (*Missionalia* 9(1981)64–78).

Takatso Mofokeng, a minister of the NG church in Africa, and lecturer at the University of Botswana, sees Black theology as a search for the meaning of Christ in the existential situation of the Blacks in South Africa. He is the author of 'A Black Christology: A New Beginning' (*Journal of Black Theology in South Africa*, first issue n.d., 1–10); 'The Evolution of the Black struggle and the Role of Black Theology' (*Conference Report on Black Theology and Black Struggle:* St Francis Xavier-Cape Town 10th–14th September 1984).

4. LIBERATION THEOLOGY

The struggle for economic and political liberation has been going on in Africa for a long time. However, it is only in the seventies that it became articulated as a theological issue, and the term 'liberation' came into Africa from Latin America.

Meinrad P. Hebga, S. J., from Cameroon, and a professor at Institut Superieur de Culture Religieuse in Abidjan, Ivory Coast, is concerned with oppressive Church structures, and advocates the emancipation of the Church in Africa from Western dominance and paternalism, and the creation of African Christian identity. He calls for a moratorium on missionaries, finance, etc., in order to allow Africans to develop their Christian identity by having direct recourse to the Christian gospels and divine revelation. His major publications include *Emancipation d'Eglises sous tutelle: Essai surl'ere post-missionaire* (Paris 1976); Sorcellerie at Prière de déliverance (Abidjan '82).

Jean-Mare Ela, another Cameroonian theologian, believes that theologising in Africa must have a grassroots basis. Thus he lives and works among the Kirdis in North Cameroon. He is concerned with politico-economic oppression as well as oppressive structures within the Church. The African church must be freed of the dependence-structures whereby it is tied to the apron strings of the Western church. He criticises political dictatorship in Africa and sees the role of the Church as prophetic in this regard. His major publications include, *African Cry* (Orbis 1986); 'Ministère ecclesial et problemes des jeunes Eglises' (*Concilium* 126 (1977) 61–69).

Englebert Mveng, S. J., of Cameroon is the general secretary of the Ecumenical Association of African theologians, and professor of history at the University of Cameroon. Mveng has introduced the concept of 'anthropological impoverishment' into African theology by which is meant that the African's poverty is a matter of 'being and non-being', rather than merely a matter of having material possession and not having it. For such a context, Marxist analysis is inadequate. He is author of 'Théologie et Langage' (*Revue Africaine De Théologie* 10 (1986) 191–208); 'Essai d'anthropologie négro – africaine: la personne humaine' (*Bulletin of African Theology* 2 (1979) 229–239); *L'art d'Afrique noire, Liturgie Cosmique et langage Religieux* (Yaounde 1974).

Laurenti Magesa, is a Catholic priest from Tanzania. He focuses on economic oppression and oppressive church structures, and uses African socialist principles to analyse the African situation in the light of the bible. He rejects capitalism and European socialism as being *institution-oriented* and against the spirit of African socialism which is *person-oriented*. He calls for a *moratorium* on missionaries, finance, etc. from abroad. His publications include *The Church and Liberation in Africa* (Eldoret, Kenya 1976), 'The Ethics of Liberation', *AFER* (1980)106–108).

Chukwudum B. Okolo is a Catholic priest and a professor at the University of Nigeria, Nsukka, Nigeria. For him liberation theology in Africa goes beyond the issue of class struggle. It involves issues of race, of oppressive church, economic and political structures, and seeks to create a better society. His publications include, *The African Church and Signs of the Times: A Socio-political Analysis* (Gaba 1978); *Marxian and Christian Ethics* (Gaba ND).

John Mutiso Mbinda, a Catholic priest from Kenya is currently the Secretary General of the Association of the Episcopal Conferences of Africa and Madagascar (AMECEA). He has advocated the application of the Harambee ideology—a Kenyan political ideology of co-operation and team work—in a theological context. Thus a political ideology and movement would form the basis of a liberation theology that would emphasise cooperation and team work. He is the author of 'Towards a Theology of Harambee' (*AFER* 20 (1978) 287–296).

Zablon Nthamburi is a Methodist minister from Kenya. He focuses on poverty and racism in South Africa, economic domination by the transnational corporations, neo-colonialism and imperialism in the Church and in theology. He offers the resurrection of Jesus as the radical symbol of Christian liberation. He is the author of 'African Theology as a Theology of Liberation' (*AFER* 22 (1980) 232–239).

Notes

1. In the Americas many authors use 'liberation theology' to refer to all Third World theologies, for example, see Deane William Ferm *Third World Liberation Theologies: An Introduction Survey* (Mary Knoll 1987).

2. See, for example, *Vie Semaine de Missiologie* (Louvaiñ1982) which carries various articles of the nature of Christian reflection on African religious thought.

3. P. D. Fueter also used it independently of Hebga in 1956. See 'Theological Education In Africa', *International Review of Missions* 27 (1956) 377ff.

Pablo Richard

The Theological Literature of Latin America

1. THE NATIONAL OR REGIONAL SOURCES OF THEOLOGICAL LITERATURE:
1980–1987

(a) Brazil

LEONARDO BOFF, a Franciscan priest, is acknowledge by the Basic Ecclesial Communities and even by the Brazilian National Episcopal Conference as the most important and creative theologian within the new model of the Church emerging in South America, which is why his three books on ecclesiology are of such note: (1) *Eclesiogénesis. Las comunidades de base reinventan la Iglesia* (Ecclesiogenesis. The Remaking of the Church by the Basic Ecclesial Communities), (2) *Iglesia: carisma y poder. Ensayo de eclesiología militante* (The Church, Charisma and Power. An Essay on Militant Ecclesiology) and (3) *Y la Iglesia se hizo pueblo. Eclesiogénesis: la Iglesia que nace de la de del pueblo* (And the Church Became a People. Ecclesiogenesis: the Church's Birth from the Faith of the People). One of Leonardo Boff's books which deals with Liberation Theology in depth and presents it in a spiritual and vigorous manner is *San Francsico de Asís: ternura y vigor* (St. Francis of Assis: His Gentleness and Strength). His creative contribution to theology also includes the feminine perspective in *El rostro materno de Dios* (The Maternal Aspect of God) and in *El Ave María. Lo femenino y el Espíritu Santo* (The Hail Mary. Femininity and the Holy Spirit). Leonardo Boff has written many works on spirituality, on the religious life and on Christology, the best of which are collected in a Spanish anthology *Jesucristo y la liberación del hombre* (Christ and the Liberation of Man).

Clodovis Boff, a Servite priest and Leonardo's brother, is also a theologian who is deeply involved with Basic Ecclesial Communities at a national level. Since the completion of his thesis *Teología y Práctica. Teología de lo político y sus mediaciones* (Theology and Practice. The Theology of Politics and its Instruments), a critical and systematic in-depth investigation of the methodology and epistemology of Liberation Theology, Clodovis Boff has published several books which examine the connection between theology and its popular base including (1) *Cómo trabajar con el pueblo. Metodología del trabajo popular* (How to Work with the People. Methodology of Working with the ·People) and (2) *Teología con los pies en la tierra* (A Theology which has its Feet on the Ground). Along with his brother Leonardo, he has played an active and public part in the latest discussions about Liberation Theology; these were (1) *La teología de la liberación en el debate actual* (Liberation Theology, the Present Debate) and (2) *Cómo hacer una teología de la liberación* (How to Construct Liberation Theology).

Frei Betto is a Dominican who has written many expository works and historical novels; he specialises in pastoral and spiritual theology. For some time he has been engaged in pastoral action amongst the workers of the industrial area of São Paulo. Recently, he has been involved in work of a political, pastoral and theological nature, both in Nicaragua and in Cuba; this work has involved the relations between Church and State and dialogue between Christian revolutionaries and Marxists. His best known book which has been widely translated is *Fidel y la religión. Conversas con Frei Betto* (Castro and Religion: Conversations with Frei Betto).

Other important figures in theology dealing with the Basic Ecclesial Communities include José Oscar Beozzo, a diocesan priest who is also an acknowledged expert on the history of the Church in Brazil, and Carlos Mesters, a Carmelite priest and the founder of the Brazilian Biblical Movement. Since the improvement in the status of women, two female theologians, Ivone Gebara (a nun working in the north-east of Brazil) and María Clara Bingemar (a married woman from Río de Janeiro) have both contributed significantly to the study of theology.

José Comblín, a Belgian theologian who has spent most of his life in Brazil and Chile, has published some 25 theological works; recently, he has placed all his learning and creativity at the service of Liberation Theology. Three of his more recent works are (1) *Tiempo de acción. Ensayo sobre el Espíritu y la historia* (A Time for Action. An Essay on the Spirit and History), (2) *El clamor de los oprimidos, el clamor de Jesús* (The Cry of the

Oppressed, the Cry of Jesus) and (3) *La fuerza de la palabra* (The Might of the Word).

Other liberation theologians in Brazil include: Hugo Assmann, Marcio Fabridos Anjos, João Batista Libanio, Gilberto Gorgulho and Julio de Santa Ana amongst others. Two laymen who have made significant contributions to the sociology of religion and are theologically involved with Basic Ecclesial Communities are Luis Alberto Gomez de Souza and Pedro Ribeiro de Oliveira. Paulo Freire, the founder of liberating pedagogy which had such an influence on Liberation Theology, also deserves mention. Many Brazilian bishops have played a prophetic and theological rôle in the liberation process—these include, amongst others, Pedro Casaldáliga, Antonio B. Fragoso, Paulo E. Arns, Aloisio Lorscheider and José M. Pires.

(b) Peru

One of the founders of Liberation Theology who will celebrate his 60th birthday this year is Gustavo Gutierrez, a diocesan priest. His two most recent works are (1) *Beber en su propio pozo. En el itinerario espiritual de un pueblo* (Drinking from One's Own Well. The Spiritual Journey of a People) and (2) *Hablar de Dios desde el sufrimiento del inocente. Un estudio Sobre Job* (The Suffering of the Innocent as Source of Talk about God. A Study of Job). Gutierrez is by far the best exponent of Liberation Theology in South America and has recently been studying spiritually and the Scriptures. Hugo Echegaray, a young priest and theologian who died in 1979, worked with Gutierrez and two of his works, published posthumously, are (1) *La práctica de Jesús* (The Practice of Jesus) and (2) *Anunciar el reino. Selección de artículos* (Proclaiming the Kingdom. A Selection of Articles.). An extensive team of theologians has come together in Lima around the person of Gutierrez; amongst them is Francisco Moreno Rejón who has published a basic work on the subject of moral theology called *Salvar la vida de los pobres. Aportes a la teología moral* (Saving the Lives of the Poor. Contributions to Moral Theology) and Manuel Diez Mateos, a biblical scholar who has begun to publish works of biblical theology in the spirit of Liberation Theology. Diego Yrarrazabal, director of the *Instituto de Estudios Aymaras* in Puno, has made a most important contribution to the study of popular religion and Andean theology. José Luis González has published a bibliography pertaining to popular religion in Lima.

Peru has also seen the publication of a series of statements by the Church in South America which have an important bearing on Liberation Theology: these are (1) *Signos de renovación* (Signs of Renewal) 1969, (2) *Signos de liberación* (Signs of Liberation) 1973, (3) *Signos de lucha y esperanza* (Signs of Struggle and Hope) 1978 and *Signos de vida y fidelidad* (Signs of Life and

Faithfulness) 1983. Very important work contributory to the popular struggle for the liberation of women within the ambit of theology has been achieved by Carmen Lora, Catalina Romero, author of *Iglesia en el Peru: compromiso y renovación* (The Church in Peru: Compromise and Renewal), Consuelo de Prado and others.

(c) Chile

Ronaldo Muñoz, a priest, has made an outstanding contribution to the study of theology relative to the Basic Ecclesial Communities in popular urban areas and the fruit of this work has been an important work on ecclesiology, *La Iglesia en el pueblo. Hacia una eclesiología latinoamericana* (The Church amongst the People. Towards a South American Ecclesiology). The specific field of Fr. José Aldunate is liberation ethics; he is also the doyen of, and the one responsible for, the formation of many Chilean theologians as well as a campaigner for the rights of the poor. Sergio Torres is a diocesan priest who has spent some fifteen years on the formation of a theology of the Third World under the aegis of the Association of Third World Theologians; a grouping of theologians from Asia, Africa, South America and from the ranks of minority groups within the USA. Segundo Galilea has written a great deal on the spirituality of liberation and he has also been involved recently in intra-ecclesial and missionary work in the Third World.

One feature of the Chilean scene has been the encouragement of lay theologians. One f these, Fernand Castillo, a sociologist and theologian, recently published a most important work, *Iglesia liberadora y política* (The Liberating and Political Church). Maximiliano Salinas is a historian who has published many works including, recently, *Historia de la Iglesia chilena desde la perspectiva de los pobres* (History of the Church in Chile from the Perspective of the Poor). Another is Manuel de Ferrari whose latest book is *Cómo leer la Biblia* (How to Read the Bible). Other lay theologians include Raúl Rosales and Christian Parker who play a crucial role in the building up of the Church of the Poor in Chile.

(d) Central America and the Caribbean

At this point in time, Nicaragua is one of the principal areas of political, ecclesial, spiritual and theological creativity in South America. These are some of the written works which reflect this reality: (1) *El Evangelio en Solentiname* (The Gospel in Solentiname) by Ernesto Cardenal, (2) *Apuntes para una teología nicaragüense* (Notes for a Nicaraguan Theology) by various authors, (3) *Fe cristiana y revolución sandinista en Nicaragua* by the various authors, (4) Teófilo Cabestrero has written several books with accounts of the spiritual and theological values of the revolution including *Ministros de Dios. Ministros del pueblo* (Ministers of God. Ministers of the People), *Revolucionarios por el Evangelio* (Revolutionaries for the Gospel), *No los separó la muerte Felipe y Mary Barreda* (Philip and Mary Barreda— Death did not Keep Them Apart) and an account of the 'evangelical uprising' in Nicaragua *Un grito a Dios y al mundo* (A Cry to God and to the World), (5) *Sandinismo, marxismo, cristianismo en la nueva Nicaragua* (Sandinism, Marxism and Christianity in a New Nicaragua) by Julio Girardi, (6) *Nicaragua: combate y profecía* (Nicaragua: Combat and Prophecy) by Pedro Casaldáliga, which is an account of the visit by this Brazilian bishop to the Church of the Poor in Nicaragua—this book is akin to hearing the Acts of the Apostles read in a contemporary context, (7) *La sangre por el pueblo. Memoria de martirio en America Latina* (Blood Spent for the People. A Record of Martyrdom in South America) is an IHCA Report, (8) *Nicaragua, trinchera teológica. Para una teología de la liberacion desde Nicaragua* (Nicaragua, A Theological Stockade. Towards a Liberation Theology from Nicaragua) by J. Girardi, B. Forcano and J. M. Vigil. In addition, the Basic Ecclesial Communities themselves have produced an impressive quantity of theology, a sure indication that even within a revolutionary process the poor people of God enjoy the capacity for reflection. Two young Nicaraguan theologians from whom much is expected in the future are José Argüello, a layman, and Napoleón Alvarado (a Jesuit priest). The following also contribute a creative and liberating theology to the revolutionary process and to the Basic Ecclesial Communities; Uriel Molina (a Franciscan), Juan Hernandez-Pico, Arnaldo Zenteno and Cesar Jerez (Jesuits), Jandir Santin, the Brazilian scripture scholar and Jorge Pixley, the well known Baptist exegetist who has recently decided to live in Nicaragua and is the author of several books on Exodus, Job and the Prophets and, lastly, Pablo Richard, the present writer, who has tried to follow the present Nicaraguan revolutionary process in his theology.

In 1987, in Cuba, a most interesting book was published called *La Iglesia católica durante la construcción del socialismo en Cuba* (The Catholic Church and the Construction of Socialism in Cuba) by Raúl Gomez Treto who is a lay lawyer. This book is an account of the process undergone by the Catholic Church from the period of confrontation to the period of dialogue with the revolution. Other important books previously published include *Cristo vivo en Cuba* (Christ Alive in Cuba) by various authors and *La herencia misionera en Cuba* (The Missionary Inheritance of Cuba), edited by R. Cepeda. At present, Cuba is undergoing a real spiritual revolution, in part due to the influence of the

Nicaraguan revolution and in part as a result of the dialogue of Church, Revolution and State. The rector of the Catholic Seminary in Havana has just published *Teología de la reconciliación* (Theology of Reconciliation).

Haiti is another focus for theological renewal where the key figure is Laennec Hurbon on account of his outstanding work on voodoo and on the black theology of liberation.

The most important theologian in El Salvador is Jon Sobrino and his latest writings include: (1) *Resurrección de la verdadera Iglesia: los pobres, lugar teológico de la eclesiología]* (Resurrection of the True Church: the Poor, the Theological Locus for Ecclesiology), (2) *Jesús en America Latina. Su significado para la fe y la cristologia* (Christ in South America. Significance for Faith and Christology) and *Liberación con Espíritu. Apuntes para una nueva espiritualidad* (Liberation and the Spirit. Notes on a New Spirituality). El Salvador is quite unique in South America for the wealth of spiritual, pastoral and theological material it has produced during these past few years. The prophetic role of Archbishop Oscar A. Romero, assassinated in 1980, grows daily and is described in *La palabra permanece: la vida de Oscar Romero* (The Word Endures: the Life of Oscar Romero) by James R. Brockman. María López Vigil has gathered together some of the spiritual wealth of the people in two books; one about a minister of the Word called Don Lito and the other about a priest called Rogelio Poncele who exercises his pastoral ministry in war areas. Another book in the same style and by an anonymous author entitled *La fe de un pueblo* (The Faith of a People) describes a ten year period in the life of a Basic Ecclesial Community.

In Costa Rica is an important regional centre, serving Central America and the Caribbean, for the theological investigation and output, for pastoral formation and for the publication of books called *El Departamento Ecuménico de Investigaciones* (The Ecumenical Research Department). Franz Hinkelammert, an economist and theologian, who has lived in South America since 1965, works there. Two of his recent publications are (1) *Las armas ideológicas de la muerte* (The Ideological Weapons of Death) and (2) *Democrácia y totalitarismo* (Democracy and Totalitarianism) and both are fundamental to the study of Liberation Theology in South America. He is presently working with Hugo Assmann, Julio de Santa Ana, Raúl Vidales and Richard Shaull on a study of economics and theology. Hinkelammert is also currently engaged in an economic and theological study of overseas debt. Another area of the study at the Ecumenical Research Department is that of the relationship between ecology and theology. At this Research Department, Carmelo Alvarez is directing a programme of re-examination of Protestant traditions from the perspectives of the poor. Pablo Richard works there in the field of biblical theology and his latest work in *La fuerza espiritual de la Iglesia de los pobres*

(The Spiritual Strength of the Church of the Poor) which carries a preface by Leonardo Boff. Elsa Tamez, a Protestant female theologian also works at this centre; she is currently studying for her doctorate in Switzerland. Since 1980, the Department has published some fifty theological works over and above the material published in the disciplines of economics, sociology and politics. Collective works published by the centre and which have had a special impact include; (1) *La lucha de los dioses. Los ídolos de la opresión y la búsqueda del Dios liberador* (The Struggle of the Gods. The Idols of Oppression and the Search for the Liberating God), (2) *Espiritualidad y Liberación en America Latina* (Spirituality and Liberation in South America) edited by E. Bonin, (3) *Cultura negra y teología* (Black Culture and Theology), (4) *El rostro femenino de la Teología* (The Female Face of Theology), (5) *Los teólogos de la liberación hablan sobre la mujer* (Liberation Theologians Discuss the Role of Women) edited by Elsa Tamez, (6) *La Iglesia de los pobres en America Central* (The Church of the poor in Central America) edited by G. Melendez and P. Richard and (7) *Raices de la teologia latinoamericana* (The Roots of South American Theology) edited by P. Richard.

(e) Mexico

The outstanding Mexican liberation theologians are the energetic Dominican priest Miguel Concha and Raúl Vidales; the latter's books include; (1) *Desde la tradición de los pobres* (From the Tradition of the Poor) and (2) *Volveré seré millones* (I Shall Return and Become Millions). Vidales has made important contributions to the methodology of Liberation Theology and is presently working on important scripts which will be published shortly on the study of Liberation Theology from the perspectives of the South American Indians. Porfirio Miranda and José Cardenas have made significant contributions to scripture studies. Marcos Villamán, a native of the Donimican Republic who works in Mexico, has written *Leyendo el Evangelio de Lucas* (Reading the Gospel of Luke). Fr. Javier Saravia is actively involved with Basic Ecclesial Communities and has published several works on the popular reading of the Bible. The Argentinian layman Enrique Dussel also lives in Mexico; he is a theologian, a philosopher and a historian and has recently been engaged in a critical revision of the works of Marx. He is both a creative and prolific writer and has just had four volumes of his more important theological writings published in Brazil entitled *Caminos de liberación latinoamericana* (The Ways to South American Liberation).

(f) Venezuela

The well known sociologist of religion and theologian Otto Maduro has published *Religión y conflicto social* (Religion and Social Conflict) which has been widely circulated and has had quite an impact throughout South America. Here, Jean-Pierre Wissenbach, Pedro Drouin and Corrado Pastore are engaged in the beginnings of biblical studies at the level of Basic Ecclesial Communities. Fr. Carlos Bazarra OFM Cap is very involved in spirituality and pastoral theology. Another source of theological output has been *El Centro Gumilla* (The Gumilla Centre) with contributions from Luis Ugalde, Mikal Munarriz, Pedro Trigo and others.

(g) Colombia

In this country the wealth of theological output from the base roots has always been repressed; knowledge of Liberation Theology is part of the oral lore. The theologian Mario Peressón runs an interesting workshop of creative theology. Alberto Parra, a Jesuit from the Xaverian University, has published *De la Iglesia misterio a la Iglesia de los pobres* (From the Church as Mystery to the Church of the Poor). Ana Maria Bidegain de Uran and Rodolfo de Roux are both well known scholars of Church history. Luis Carlos Bernal, Federico Carrasquilla, Hector Torres and the female theologian Carmiña Navia work with Basic Ecclesial Communities. The Claretian, Gonzalo de la Torre, is a well known scripture scholar and we look forward to his next writings.

(h) The Argentine and Urauguay

The Argentine is just emerging from the dark night of terror and dictatorship in which Liberation Theology was repressed both by the political and ecclesiastical authorities. Yet, despite all that, Severino Croatto has managed to be a most creative scripture scholar and has completed important studies of the Book of Genesis and recently published *Hermenéutica bíblica* (Biblical Hermeneutics). José Miguez Bonino enjoys universal acclaim for his work on Liberation Theology. Quite recently, Ana María Ezcurra returned to the Argentine, as did Ruben Dri who had published in Mexico *La Utopía de Jesus* (Utopia of Jesus). The best known writer in this field in Uraguay is Juan Luis Segundo who is noted for his profundity, his creativity and his erudition. He has presented a highly developed synthesis of Liberation Theology in his *El hombre de hoy ante Jesús de Nazaret* (Contemporary Man Face to Face with Jesus of Nazereth) which consists of three volumes; and, equally important is his *Teología de la liberación: Respuesta al Cardenal Ratzinger* (Liberation Theology: a reply to Cardinal Ratzinger).

(i) Ecuador, Bolivia and Paraguay

In Ecuador, a very creative theologian working with Basic Ecclesial Communities has been Fr. José Luis Caravias who has many published works to his credit. Fr. Victor Codina has carried out the same kind of work in Bolivia after having worked many years in Europe; his principal writings are (1) ¿Qué es la Teología de la Liberación? (What is Liberation Theology?), (2) Teología del clamor popular (Theology of the People's Outcry) and (3) De la modernidad a la solidaridad (From Modernness to Solidarity). Also in Bolivia, Fr. Gregorio Iriarte, along with an impressive team of anthropologists and theologians, has been working at the development of a Liberation Theology from the perspectives of the native Indian peoples of South America. Paraguay is undergoing a collective martyrdom under the oldest dictatorship in South America. Undoubtedly, a very important Liberation Theology will be the eventual fruit of that situation.

2. THE SUBCONTINENTAL THEMES AND SUBJECT MATTERS OF THEOLOGICAL
LITERATURE

(a) Liberation Theology from the Native Indian Perspective

One of the greatest challenges facing Liberation Theology is that in 1992 the 500th. anniversary of the evangelisation of South America will be 'celebrated'. In this respect, a most important book is Aporte de los pueblos indígenas de America Latina a la teología cristiana (The Contribution of the Indian Peoples of South America to Christian Theology) which was published in Quito in 1986. Two historical studies by Fernando Mires are equally important En nombre de la cruz (In the Name of the Cross) published by DEI in 1986 and La colonización de las almas (The Colonising of Souls) published by DEI in 1987. Pioneering work of an enduring nature has been carried out in Brazil by Paulo Suess, see Culturas indigenas y evangelización (Evangelisation and the Native Cultures) and by CIMI, El Consejo Indigenista Misionero (The Indian Missionary Council), of the Brazilian Episcopal Conference. Similarly, in Peru we have El Instituto de Pastoral Andina (The Andean Pastoral Institute) based in Sicuani and El Instituto de Estudios Aymaras (The Institute for Aymaran Studies) based in Puno, where the theologian Diego Yrarrázabal works. The Jesuit anthropologist, B. Melía, has published in Brazil a book about Paraguay with a preface by Pedro Casaldáliga entitled En busca de la tierra sin mal (In Search of a Land without Evil). CEHILA (see infra) has also published a great quantity of material on the same subject.

(b) Liberation Theology from the Black Perspective

This particular theme also presents a most important challenge for Liberation Theology in South America. In this respect, the Conference of 25 black theologians from South America and from the Caribbean which took place in Rìo de Janeiro in July 1985 is of crucial importance. The papers of this conference were published in Spanish and in Portuguese *Cultura negra y teología* (Black Culture and Theology). Laennec Hurbon, in Haiti, and Quince Duncan, in Costa Rica, are both pioneers in this particular field. The black Capuchin priest Agustín Sambola is making important contributions to the study of black theology in Nicaragua. An important centre of creative work in this field is CESEP, *Centro Ecuménico de Servicios para la Evangelización y la Educación Popular* (Ecumenical Centre for Services to Popular Evangelisation and Education) in São Paulo where the young black theologian Marcos Rodrigeuz da Silva works as does José Oscar Beozzo, the theologian who has conducted the most thorough theoretical and historical research on this subject.

(c) Liberation Theology from the Perspective of Women

The emergence of women in the Church and in theology is one of the most powerful signs of hope for the future of South America. The South American Conference on Liberation Theology from the Perspective of Women, held in Buenos Aires in November 1985, was a watershed in this particular field. Twenty-eight women theologians from South America and the Caribbean took part in this conference and the conference papers were published under the title *El rostro femenino de la teología* (The Feminine Face of Theology) (San José, 1986) and also appeared in the first six months' issue of *Revista Eclesiástica Brasilera* (Brazilian Ecclesiastical Review) in 1986. These publications included the writings of Ivone Gebara (a Brazilian nun), of María Clara Bingemar (a Brazilian lay women) and of Elsa Tamez (a Protestant lay woman from Mexico) who are the better known women liberation theologians. Special importance has to be given to the summary documents from this conference. Other well-known women theologians who have published important works include Teresa Cavalcanti, Alida Verhoeven, Nelly Ritchie, Carmiña Navia, Carmen Lora and Catalina Romero. Native Indian women who have contributed notably to this discipline include Domitila from Bolivia and Rigoberta Menchu from Guatemala. The works of Julia Esquival from Guatemala, both in poetry and in prose, must be taken into account in this particular respect along with the many book written about the rôle played by women in the Sandinist Revolution. Many other crucial written works have emerged from Chile and from the Argentine.

(d) **The Writing of Church History from the Perspective of the Poor**

CEHILA, *La Comisión de Estudios de Historia de la Iglesia Latino-americana* (The Commission for the Study of the History of the Church in South America) has made the most important contribution to this particular subject to date: Enrique Dussel is president of CEHILA at this time. Some fifty specialist scholars are engaged in the re-writing of church history from the perspective of the Indians, the blacks and the oppressed in general with an overview of the economic, political and cultural contexts of the Church as the People of God. Historians working along these lines include José Oscar Beozzo, Eduardo Hoornaert, Ana María Bidegain de Uran, Rodolfo de Roux, Samuel Silva Gotay, Mazimiliano Salinas, Guillermo Meléndez, Miguel Picado, Pablo Richard and others. Six volumes of a General History of the Church have already appeared covering Mexico, Central America, Venezuela and Colombia, Brazil (2 volumes), and an introductory volume on Hispanics in the USA. Other projects include short histories of each country, a history of religious life, a history of theology and a popular history of the Church.

(e) **The Popular Reading of the Bible**

Two South American Conferences have already taken place in an attempt to organise the work of exegetics' experts who are liberationist in regard to hermeneutics and who encourage the reading of the Bible within the Basic Ecclesial Communities. The inspiration behind this effort is Carlos Mesters whose most recent publication is *Flor sin defensa. Una explicación de la Biblia a partir del pueblo* (A Defenceless Flower. A Popular Interpretation of the Bible). In Brazil, there is in operation a far-reaching biblical movement amongst the people and Milton Schwantes, Gilberto Gorgulho, Ana Flora Anderson, Marcelo de Barros Souza and others work together on this project which has already seen a steady growth in Chile, Peru, Central America and in Mexico. Other South American biblical scholars engaged in this kind of work include José Cardenas in Mexico, Pablo Richard in Central America, Severino Croatto in the Argentine, Jorge Pixley in Nicaragua and others. Work is well in hand on *Comentario Bíblico Latinoamericano* (South American Biblical Commentary) and ten volumes have appeared to date. In 1980 the first issue of *Revista de Interpretación Bíblica Latino-americana* (Review of South American Biblical Interpretation) was published both in Spanish and in Portuguese.

(f) **Liberation Theology: Systematic and Collective Effort**

Some 60 theologians of both sexes from all over the subcontinent have come together to develop the first general synthesis of South American theology which will be published simultaneously in Spanish and in Portuguese. The general title of this work is *Teología y liberación* (Theology and Liberation). It is hoped that translations will follow into English, German, Italian, French etc. and the following parts have already been published: (1) *La memoria del pueblo cristiano* (The Memory of the Christian People) by E. Hoornaert, (2) *Opción por los pobres* (Option for the Poor) by C. Boff and J. Pixley, (3) *Dios de los cristianos* (The God of Christians) by R. Muñoz, (4) *La Trinidad, la sociedad y la liberación* (The Trinity, Society and Liberation) by L. Boff, (5) *Antropología cristiana* (Christian Anthropology) by J. Comblin, (6) *Etica comunitaria* (Community Ethics) by E. Dussel, (7) *Escatología Cristiana* (Christian Eschatology) by Libanio and Bingemer, (8) *La doctrina social de la Iglesia* (The Social Teaching of the Church) by Antoncich and Munariz, (9) *Ecumenismo y liberación* (Ecumenism and Liberation) by Julio de Santa Ana, (10) *El Espíritu Santo y la liberación* (The Holy Spirit and Liberation) by J. Comblin, (11) *Teología moral: impases y alternativas* (Moral Theology: Impasses and Alternatives) by Moser and Leers, (12) *Sacramento, praxis y fiesta* (Sacramento, Practice and Festival) by F. Taborda, (13) *Vida religiosa—historia y teología* (Religious Life—History and Theology) and (14) *Maria: mujer del pueblo y Madre de Dios* (Mary, Mother of the People and Mother of God) by Gebara and Bingemer. By the time this issue of Concilium appears in print, some 10 other titles will have been added to that list.

(g) Magazines and Reviews Dedicated to Liberation Theology

The shortage of space demands that these be simply named along with their place of publication: *Paginas* (Pages), Lima; *Pastoral Popular* (People's Pastoral), Santiago; *Christus*, Mexico; *Servir* (To Serve), Jalapa, Mexico; *Christianismo y Sociedad* (Christianity and Society), Mexico; *Perspectiva Teologica* (Theological Perspective), Belo Horizonte; *Revista Eclesiastica Brasileira* (Brazialian Ecclesiastical Review), Petropolis; *Teologia Latinoamericana* (South American Theology), El Salvador; *Carta a las Iglesias* (Letter to the Churches), El Salvador; *Pasos* (Steps), San José, Costa Rica; *Diakonia*, Managua; *Amenecer* (Dawn), Managua; *Solidaridad* (Solidarity), Bogota; *Cencos-Iglesia* (Cencos-Church), Mexico; *Sic*, Caracas; *Ribla*, Brazil and Costa Rica; *Caminos de Encuentro* (Roads to Encounter), Buenos Aires; *Pastoral Andina* (Andean Pastoral), Sicuani, Peru; *Iglesia y Pueblo* (Church and People), La Paz; *Dialogo Social* (Social Dialogue), Panama; *Biblito*, Santiago; and others.

(h) Theological Institutions Dedicated to Liberation Theology

A feature of the South American scene has been the appearance of centres where theology is studied in a collective, multidisciplined and ecumenical way. Many of these centres conduct workshops and courses of formation for Basic Ecclesial Communities and engage in publishing. They are genuine 'collective and organic theological institutions'. I draw the reader's attention to some of these: *Centro Ecuménico Diego de Medellin* (The Diego de Medellin Ecumenical Centre), Chile; *Centro Bartolomé de las Casas* (The Bartolome de las Casas Centre), Lima; *Encuentro Cristiano* (Christian Encounter), Cediq and *Centro Nazaret* (Nazereth Centre), Argentine; *CESEP—Centro Ecuménico de Servicios para la Evangelización y la Educación Popular* (Ecumenical Centre for Services in Popular Evangelisation and Education), São Paulo; *CEBI—Centro de Estudios Bíblicos* (Biblical Studies Centre), São Paulo; *CEDI—Centro Ecuménico de Investigaciones* (Ecumenical Research Centre), São Paulo; *DEI— Departamento Ecuménico de Investigaciones* (Ecumenical Research Department), *Centro Ecuménico Antonio de Valdivieso* (The Antonio de Valdivieso Ecumenical Centre), *CEPA—Centro de Evangelizacion y Pastoral Agraria* (Centre for Agrarian Pastoral and Evangelisation), *Instituto Histórico Centro Americano* (The Central American Historical Institute), all in Managua; *Centro Antonio de Montesinos* (The Antonio de Montesinos Centre), Mexico; and many more. *CLAR—Conferencia Latinoamericana de Religiosos* (South American Conference of Religious), particularly through the agency of its own theologians, has proved to be an important source of theology for the whole of South America.

CONCLUSION

In conclusion, I wish to point out that all these theologians, books, reviews and magazines, and theological centres are only the *branches* of a great *tree*. The *trunk* which gives life to these *branches* and sustains them consists of the Basic Ecclesial Communities and the *roots* from which the sap and energy which feed the whole come are the religious and spiritual life of the poor and believing people of South America. In order to understand and get to know Liberation Theology in South America it is necessary to know the *whole tree*; *roots, trunk* and *branches*. The vital strength of Liberation Theology lies in the fact that it is *rooted* in the life of the poor people of God; in their spirituality and in their Basic Ecclesial Communities and that is where we have to find our strength and our future. Liberation Theology also finds a *universality* in dialogue with the theologies of liberation of Africa, Asia, Europe and the USA. Finally, from the spiritual and historical strengths of the poor and the oppressed, the

Liberation Theology of South America will continue to grow as it serves to renew the Church spiritually and institutionally.

Translated by John Angus Macdonald

Note

All English versions of Spanish titles and proper names have been provided by the translator for the guidance of the English reader. They do not indicate existing English titles.

Dorothy Folliard

Theological Literature of the USA Minorities

THE THEOLOGICAL literature coming out of the struggles of the racial/ethnic minorities of the USA is just beginning. In this brief bibliography, we will seek to merely point out the names of some of the more creative thinkers that we have encountered. There are many more and hopefully, still many more will emerge in the years to come. In solidarity with other oppressed brothers and sisters of the Third World, these minority spokespersons are seeking to create something new. They do not want to simply repeat the theological discourse of the past. They do not see it as pastorally relevant—either then, or today, either in Euro-North America or anywhere else. Hence they seek to create a theology in communion with their peoples which will be truly faithful to the Gospel by being relevant to life, its ultimate meaning and its destiny in the context of today's burning questions and issues. We will limit ourselves to the three predominant minorities of the USA: the Blacks, the Hispanics and the Native Americans, because these have been and continue to be the poorest, the most oppressed, and the most exploited.

The existence of Black colleges and Black churches with Blacks being their own professors, pastors and pastoral agents in Protestantism has contributed greatly to today's existence of Black thought and theological reflection. The other minorities, especially within the Catholic community, have not had the luxury of having their own colleges and being pastors of their own people. For the most part, Hispanics and Native Americans are still being served by ministers who are foreigners to them. They have not had the opportunity of ministering to their own within their churches nor of developing their own religious thought. Hence it is not surprising that the Blacks have taken the leadership in reflecting theologically out of their unique experience of slavery, suffering and exploitation.

1. BLACK LITERATURE

When one thinks of Black in the USA, one immediately thinks of such great names as Martin Luther King, Jr, Malcolm X and Jesse Jackson: three powerful symbols of non-violent Christian power, pride and self-defence—and the political-practical transformation of society. These great persons have a tremendous impact not just on the Blacks, but on the whole of the USA Church and Society.

Amongst the theologians who are reflecting critically about the Christian meaning of the Black experience in the United States, the name of James Cone immediately stands out not only as one of the truly creative pioneers of Black theology but equally as one who continues to deepen and expand the meaning and mission of Black religion. His own personal association with other theologians of the Third World has allowed Black thought both to enrich and be enriched by the theological reflection of other peoples who have likewise suffered oppression and domination. He is professor of Systematic Theology at Union Theological Seminary in New York. Chief among his published works include such titles as *Black Theology and Black Power* (1969); *A Black Theology of Liberation* (1970); *The Spirituals and the Blues: An interpretation* (1972); *The God of the Oppressed* (1975); *Black Theology: A documentary History, 1966-79* (edited with Gayraud S. Wilmore, 1979); *For My People* (1984); and *Speaking the Truth* (1986). He is presently working on a book soon to be published on Martin Luther King, Jr, and Malcolm X. He has also published numerous articles and presently is more and more involved in inter-relating Black thought with the Third World theologies of Africa, Latin America and Asia.

Other major authors arising out of the Black experience include such persons as Albert B. Cleage *The Black Messiah* (1968); J. Deotis Roberts *Liberation and Reconciliation: A Black Theology* (1971); Major J. Jones *Black Awareness: A Theology of Hope* (1971); and Gayraud S. Wilmore *Black Religion and Black Radicalism* (1972). One of the most creative and serious of the new Black Theologians who are emerging is Cornel West with his far-reaching book *Prophesy Deliverance* (1982).

Black women theologians are equally beginning to emerge with creative and provocative persons such as Delores Williams, Kelly Brown, Jackie Grant, Cheryl Townsend and Katie Cannon.

Whereas Protestant Black theologians had been almost the exclusive voice of the Blacks, new voices are beginning to emerge out of the Catholic Black experience of the USA. The most promising and creative is Edward Braxton who has published extensively on the Black Catholic experience in the USA. He is a theological consultant for a major religious education series (Sadlier of New York) and as such has impact not only on Black Catholics but on all Catholics of the English speaking world. Some of the other authors who have begun to emerge include Cyprian Davis of St Meinard School of Theology, Bishop James P. Lyke, Shaun Copeland, Thea Bowman and Janie Phelps. Even though Black Catholics are just beginning to speak and write about their situation, they are already having a major impact on the US Catholic Church.

2. HISPANIC LITERATURE

The most important persons who best symbolise the life and struggles of the Hispanics in the United States are Caesar Chavez who has led the prophetic struggle of the United Farm Workers, Archbishop Patrick F. Flores who became the first Hispanic bishop of United States and who has dedicated his life to the struggles of his people and the late Willie Velasquez who gave his life to the political awakening of the Hispanics in this country. These are the persons who stand as the light upon the mountain top giving light and direction to the Hispanic movements of the USA.

Amongst the Hispanic thinkers, the first theological literature started with Virgil Elizondo's *Christianity and Culture* (1975) which was an early attempt to carry out the teachings of the missionary decree of Vatican II in relation to the Mexican Americans of the United States. This was the first book which marked both the continuity and the break with Latin American thought. It presented the Hispanics of the USA as a distinct group which had the privilege and responsibility of producing its own theological works.

Since then, he has published numerous other works dealing with the question of socio-cultural oppression, evangelisation and liberation. Among his more popular works one can find *La Morenita: Evangeliser of the Americas* (1980) which re-reads the Guadalupe apparitions from the perspective of the native Indians to whom she appeared; *Virgen y Madre* (1983) which studies Marian devotion from the life parallels of Mary of Nazareth and poor women of society; and his best known *Galilean Journey; The Mexican American Promise* (1983), in which he does a cultural reading of the Gospel so that he may then do a Gospel reading of the culture. This book is a real breakthrough in pastoral hermeneutics and even though it speaks specifically of the Mexican American experience, it is a model that can certainly serve other groups in the universal Church. His latest book is a good example of story theology as he theologises out of his own life history in the context of the history of his people: *L'avenir est au métissage* (1986). This book was beautifully prefaced by the late Léopold Sédar Senghor. He has published a great number of articles in major periodicals on the question of Gospel and culture. Elizondo continues to be the most creative and prophetic voice of the Hispanics of the USA.

Collaborating closely with Elizondo through the Mexican American Cultural Centre is a team of theologians who, although they are not Hispanics by birth, nevertheless are doing some very creative theologising from amongst the Hispanic American experience. John Linskens is a Dutch born New Testament scholar. Juan Alfaro is a Spanish born Old Testament scholar who also works on the writings of John; and Dorothy Folliard is Irish Chicago born with a speciality in contemporary Protestant theologies. Others who have contributed to the development of the literature include the Cuban born Justo Gonzalez and the Mexican born Jorge Lara Braud. Both have contributed significantly within the Protestant religious experience.

New important contributions are beginning to come forth among the young generation of theologians. Rosendo Urrabazo who recently succeeded Virgil Elizondo as President of the Mexican American Cultural Centre is developing new knowledge in the fields of family values and the inter-relationship betweeen church and politics. Allen Figuroa Deck heads the new Hispanic Studies programme at the Jesuit School of Theology at Berkeley. He has written some very good articles on the theology of migration and is beginning to explore in co-operation with theologians from Mexico new ways of doing theology. Andres Guerrero is beginning to develop the theology of the Chicano movement.

David Abalos, who is professor of Religious Studies and Sociology at Seton Hall University, explores the interrelationship between the sacred and the political in his recent book *Latinos in the United States* (1986). Another important name in this area is Gilbert Cadena who just completed his doctoral dissertation with a thesis on *Chicanos and the Catholic Church: Liberation Theology as a Form of Empowerment* (1987).

In the field of worship there are such persons as Rosa Maria Icaza, Arturo Perez, and Juan Sosa. In the field of folk religion and ministry Maria de la Cruz Aymes, Angela Ereyia and Dororita Martinez are making some interesting explorations. In the field of systematic theology we are beginning to develop our first theologians with Roberto Goizueta of Emory University in the field of international economics and Christian ethics, Orlando Espin and Sixto Garcia of St Vicent de Paul Regional Seminary in Florida are working on the Afro-Hispanic religious experience of the USA. Gilbert Romero of Los Angeles is working on the field of biblical perspectives of popular religiosity. Tony Stevens Arroyo continues to be the most creative of the Puerto Rican writers.

In the field of women and religion, Maria Pilar Aquina is beginning some serious work, as is Soledad Galleron. Also someone like Jeanette Rodrigeuz Holguin is a good example of a new type of theologian: she is a wife, a mother, a pastoral worker and a theologian. But the best breakthrough by two very creative, serious and prophetic women is the recently published book *Hispanic Women: Prophetic Voice in the Church* (1987) written by Yolanda Tarrango (Mexican American) and Ada Maria Isasi Diaz (Cuban born/USA).

One of the most interesting breakthroughs of Hispanic thought are the *Conclusions of the 3rd National Meeting of USA Hispanic Catholics* where a team has worked together to gather the various opinions of participants from throughout the country who themselves had participated in intense listening projects in their own respective areas. The people have spoken— and out of their collective voice, the US Catholic Bishops have put together a national pastoral plan for Hispanics. This represents a totally new way of developing pastoral plans. There is a fascinating ecclesiology underlying this new process of the entire People of God—pastors and people— working together to reflect critically on the meaning of our faith.

3. NATIVE AMERICAN LITERATURE

The native Americans have been in these lands the longest; and equally has their suffering been the most prolonged. To a large degree they are still being ministered to, but seldom participate fully in either ministry or the development of their own theological Christian thought. For the native Americans, 1992 will be the commemoration of 500 years of slow and systematic ethnocide and genocide. Their silence and regular absence from gathering of the poor and the suffering of our country in itself is a powerful message!

Vine Deloria, Jr has been one of the most vociferous and prophetic voices to come out of the Native Americans. He has published *Custor Died for Your Sins* (1969); *We Talk, You Listen* (1970); and *God is Red* (1973). Robert S. Michaelson has published 'We also Have a Religion: the Free Exercise of Religion among Native Americans' in the *American Indian Quarterly* (no 3, 1983) and Clifford Trafzer wrote 'American Indian Prophets: religious leaders and revitalization movements' also published in the *American Indian Quarterly* (no 3, 1985).

Other native Americans who are beginning to relate Christian thought and their own experience are Mike Galvan, Genevieve Cumy and Kateri Mitchell. Working with them and reflecting out of what they have learned by living and working among the Native Americans one finds Gilbert Hemauer who has written *A Cross-Cultural approach to catechetics* (1977); *The Process of Inculturation: Ways of sharing the Catholic Way* (1977). Carl Starkloff has written *American Indian Religion and Christianity: Confrontation and Dialogue* (1971); and *Native Spirituality and Christian Stewardship* (1981). Michael Stettenkamp wrote *Sacred Vision* (1982); and William Stolzman wrote *The Pipe and Christ* (1986). These works written by non-Native Americans who immersed themselves in the ways of Native Americans no longer seek to justify the Western religious domination through so-called conversion to Christianity but truly see evangelisation in the style of Vatican II: as the walking along with a people, discovering with them the Gospel whose very seeds already lie within the native ways and culture. In this new evangelising process, the missioner himself/herself is evangelised and changed by the very people they are serving.

One can easily keep up with what is coming out of Native American thought through the *Tekawitha Conference Newsletter* (PO Box 6759 Great Falls, MT 59406, USA).

This short bibliographical summary is intended to give only representative references to published works from these three minorities and to name some of those engaged in this reflective process. To be a truly complete report, one would have to hear the quiet voices of those who have no access to publication but who continue to support one another in faith as they glorify the God of life. Even in the most oppressive situations within a dominant society that continues to ignore their prophetic message, they sing their songs and proclamations of liberation and new life.

Hyung-Kung Chung

Opium or the Seed for Revolution?: Shamanism: Women Centred Popular Religiosity in Korea

SHAMANISM (MUSOK) is the 'women-centred' popular religiosity that is widely practised among poor people in Korea. Is it a revolutionary seed that empowers both Christians and non-Christians to fight for their liberation or is it a sedative which makes them accept their situation of oppression?

For many years, many educated people in Korea despised Shamanism as 'opium of the poor'. They referred to it as a superstitious religious practice which provided 'ignorant people' (especially 'emotional women') with an escape from the *real world*. It could not, therefore, provide any revolutionary impetus for socio-political changes in Korean society.

Recently, however, another interpretation of Shamanism has emerged in Korea. Korean young workers, farmers, and students in the liberation movements have begun to use Shamanistic ritual (*kut*) as one of the most important tools for their movement. They perform the *kut* in the midst of their demonstrations against the dictatorial government, US imperialism, and multi-national corporations. As Christians invite the Holy Spirit to be present

---

Note: Since Tissa Balasuriya has already presented the reader with many of the names of the new theologians, we include a concrete example of one new style of doing theology in one country of Asia.

with them in worship and in times of distress, farmers, young workers and students offer a similar invitation to the *Han*-ridden ghosts at the beginning of the *Kut*.[1] These ghosts are the spirit of the people who died from sickness or were killed unjustly in the liberation movement without seeing the 'New World' they dreamed of in Korean history. The demonstrators offer food, dance, song and prayer to the *Han*-ridden ghosts so that the latter will empower the former in their struggle against the forces of oppression. According to the demonstrators, *Kut* is the most nationalistic Minjung ritual which is not from the colonialists' religion, such as Christianity.[2]

Some Korean theologians also have begun to appropriate Shamanistic resources in their attempt to develop a theology out of everyday life experiences of the oppressed Minjung. They contend that the world of the Minjung can be taken seriously only to the degree that the religion of the Minjung (Shamanism) is *appropriated as the main source* for their theology.

Not surprisingly, many Korean women—especially participants in women's liberation movements or in Women's Studies—also turn to Shamanism as a source of power. They contend that Shamanism is the only religious context where women's power and leadership has been sustained throughout Korean history, providing women-centred space within a patriarchal society.

It seems that a new Shamanistic Renaissance has emerged among justice concerned people in Korea. As a Korean woman who feels compelled to do theology in the context of the Korean people's movement, I have naturally nurtured my interest in Korean Shamanism. This natural interest has become a passionate obsession. It began a few years ago after I heard the news that my high school friend, Jiheh, had become an initiated Shaman (*Mudang*), largely influenced by her participation in the student movement.[3] I sometimes feel almost possessed by her being. But then I realise that she is not an *object* for my observation. Rather, she is a *person*, a *comrade* who, like me, is deeply concerned about the liberation of our homeland.

My theological journey as a Third World woman prepared me for my recent encounter with Jiheh as a Shaman. As Aloysius Pieris has said, 'the irruption of the Third World is also the irruption of the non-Christian world'.[4] This is particularly true for Asia. If we, as Third World theologians, expect to create a theology that is faithful to the liberation struggle of the poor, then we must listen to and learn from the religion of the non-Christian poor, which is also *the religion from the underside of religion*. In doing this, we should also remember that women are the majority of the poor who actively participate in creating and nurturing popular religiosity.

Shamanism in Korea was considered *devil worship* by western missionaries. It was regarded as animistic, primitive and thus an inferior religion because it focused on women's mundane life and *the earth*. Shamanism was often considered as a-historical, a-moral cosmic religion which had to be *corrected*, that is, *domesticated* by the higher, male-centred, meta-cosmic religions.

To learn about Shamanism, therefore, is to encounter a typical woman-centred religion from the underside of the dominant world religions. Third World theologians' study of Shamanism should not be out of mere curiosity. It is a necessity for all who have genuine interest in the people who are the most hurt and oppressed and who are determined to be liberated from their bondage.

1. THEOLOGICAL PRESUPPOSITIONS

Before searching for the liberating impetus of Shamanism, it is necessary to make my theological presuppositions explicit.

First, my interpretation is 'gender specific'—that is, defined by women's experience. *Third World women suffer because they are poor.* While their suffering includes material poverty, it is more than that. Third World Women are poor because they are not treated as equal partners in the human community. That was why Mercy Oduyoye named women's reality as an 'irruption within the irruption',[5] a reality that EATWOT men found difficult to understand and to incorporate into their theology. Women also resonate with the feeling of 'the anthropological poverty' that Englebert Mveng expressed as an African at the Fifth Assembly of EATWOT in New Delhi.[6] Many male theologians often talk about the poor. But as Third World women, we frequently feel that they are talking about poor *men* and not necessarily poor *women*. Therefore, in order to make the voices of women heard, we must emphasise the 'female gender specificity' in our definition of the meaning of suffering and liberation.

Second, my interpretation of Korean Shamanism is also defined by the contemporary People's Movement for liberation in Korea. This means that my interpretation of the 'liberating' and 'oppressive' dimensions of Shamanism is made through the eyes of the people who are participating in the Third World liberation struggle. In other words, I intentionally limit my examination of Shamanism to those aspects which liberation activists find useful and will not, in this essay, be concerned with characteristics which the observers of the struggle define as negative. I believe that the 'liberating' and 'alienating' aspects of Shamanism can only be judged by those who are actively seeking to establish justice in society. They may be nationalistic students, farmers, workers, religious persons (especially women), or *anybody who is at the front line of the movement for liberation and self-determination of our people.*

Third, my interpretation of Shamanism is shaped by my commitment to the Christian Gospel. By birth I *became* a Christian, and by choice I decided to *remain* a Christian, but not without a difference. My perspective on the Christian Gospel is not defined by the particular missionary brand that initially introduced me to Jesus Christ. Rather it has been carved out of my solidarity with the struggle of Koreans and other Third World people for liberation. This liberation struggle is not separate from the movement of freedom that has also inspired a new liberation impetus in Shamanism. Therefore, liberation-centred Christianity and liberation-centred Shamanism are not totally separate realities. In some sense they are *one* reality that empowers the poor to fight for justice and freedom.

Because Christianity and Shamanism are linked together in the democratic struggle in Korea, I have chosen to speak of a kind of 'liberation-centred syncretism'. In their struggle for justice, poor people come to many different religious sources for sustenance and empowerment. What matters for the people are not Christian doctrines in contrast with Shamanist beliefs. What matters is *liberation of the people from bondage!* What matters is not Jesus or Buddha or General Choi Young[7] or Samshin Grandmother,[8] but rather *the spirit of liberation* which empowers the people to claim self-determination for themselves.

Fourth, Shamans and Shamanistic believers (the majority of whom are women), must be encountered as *subjects* and not as *objects for observation.* In male-centred traditions, women have been observed as merely objects and in relation to the interests of men. In academic discourse and general public definitions of religion and culture, male hegemony presupposes that a woman is defined by her *relationship to men*—father, brother, husband, or son. However, I agree with other Third World women who say that *our reality must be defined by ourselves.* As Sun-Ai Park has said, 'neither Third World men nor First World women can determine the Third World women's agenda'[9] *We are the subjects of our own history.*

In order to meet the Shamans and Shamanist believers *as subjects*, it is important to encounter a 'socio-biography'[10] of a young Shaman in the movement: my honourable high school friend, Jiheh.

2. JIHEH'S SOCIO-BIOGRAPHY: A PROTOTYPE OF A NEW GENERATION OF SHAMAN IN THE LIBERATION MOVEMENT

When I first heard about Jiheh's story six years ago I was shocked. I could not believe what happened to her. *She had become a Shaman!* I thought it could not be true because the majority of Shamans in Korea were considered to be ignorant, superstitious women. Jiheh did not fit that image. During our high school years, she was a brilliant and talented student. Writer, painter and ballet dancer, Jiheh excelled in many things and was greatly admired by many people.

As most people who knew her expected, Jiheh entered one of the most élite art colleges in Korea. During our college years, we lost contact. She became an active participant in the student movement. It soon became clear to her that the Western art, which she studied in school, could not serve as an effective tool for the liberation of the Korean people. She dropped out of college and started to collect Korean Minjung art forms—especially songs and dances from the grass-roots people.

While Jiheh was collecting art forms, she became sick. The reason for her illness was unclear. One day she went to a Shaman's place to learn Korean Shaman dance. The Shaman, however, recognised that Jiheh was suffering with possession sickness (*Sinbyong*), a common occurrence in persons before they become an initiated Shaman. Initially, Jiheh strongly resisted her 'calling' as a Shaman. Her western training hindered her appreciation of Shamanism. However, eventually she decided to become a Shaman, and her illness disappeared.

After becoming an initiated Shaman, Jiheh gave an interview for a women's magazine in which she revealed her family background. Jiheh's mother conceived her with a man who deceived her. He told Jiheh's mother that he was a bachelor, and he persuaded her to develop a serious relationship with him. However, when Jiheh was born and had to be registered as *his* child (according to patrilineal Korean social law), he refused to acknowledge her publicly as his daughter. Jiheh's mother found out that he was a married man with a family of his own. Therefore, Jiheh had to take her mother's last name, which was very scandalous in terms of Korean culture. Because she was conceived in deception, rejected by her father, and raised with the name of her mother, Jiheh embodied Korean women's *Han*.

Jiheh's activities as a Shaman have been very *socially* oriented. The day that a Korean women's liberation organisation (Yeo Sung Pyung Wo Hoe) was founded, she performed the *Kut* to bless the group. She celebrated women's power by dancing on a sharp sword while holding her infant daughter. She also performed *Kut* in front of a factory while women workers demonstrated against multi-national corporations. According to some people's testimony, she exorcised capitalism, multi-national corporations and military dictatorships. They contend that her guiding spirit is the spirit of the *Baek-Du* mountain, located on the boundary of North Korea and

China. Some people believe that the *Baek-Du* mountain spirit will guide Jiheh in her work toward the unification of Korea by casting out the evil ghost of imperialism.

3. SHAMAN AS A PRIESTESS OF 'HAN'

Jiheh's initiation into Shamanhood can be interpreted as the symbolic embodiment of young liberationists' historical consciousness. Most persons who accept this interpretation are young people whom I call 'second generation liberationists'. 'First generation liberationists' experienced *Japanese colonialism*, the *division of the nation*, and the *Korean War*. They worked hard to save our country from these tragedies. Their main concern was 'nation building'—emphasising the need for education, development, and modernisation. The first generation liberationists were critical of the behaviour and culture of the Minjung, since the latter's 'ignorance' seemed to hinder the advancement of Korean society into the modern world.

The 'second generation liberationists' were born *after independence from Japan* after independence from Japan and have become disillusioned by the first generationists' promises of freedom which education and modernisation were intended to achieve for Korean people. The people who received most of the benefits of the western-style education and modernisation were a few power élites who had direct connections with neo-colonial power. The majority of *Minjung*—the poor people of Korea—remained in poverty.

As second generation liberationists realised the great limitations of modernisation, they began to ask, 'where do we turn for the power of liberation?' It seemed clear to them that the people responsible for creating the great gap between the rich and poor in Korea simply would not provide the tools to effect radical changes in the society. The place to turn then was to the wisdom of the people at the bottom—the *Minjung*. Our generation has come to know that *Minjung* are the real subject of the history of liberation and not a small élite. This understanding encouraged many educated young people to learn their history, culture and religion—humbly—from the *Minjung*. Now we see many young people learning maal dances, farmer's dances, orally inherited songs and learning how to play traditional Korean instruments.

Buddhist, Confucianism, and Christianity are *imported religions* in Korea. They have been used by the ruling élite to maintain the *status quo*. Shamanism, however, was not imported but was created out of the people's lives. Some young people define Shamanistic ritual, *Kut*, as both the community organisation of the *Minjung* and a celebration of the hope derived from their refusal to bow down to the forces of oppression.[11] Through historical research, direct connections have been discovered between Shamanism and many *Minjung* revolutionary movements in Korea. By becoming a Shaman, it could be said that Jiheh embodied the consciousness of these young liberationists.

Who are the Shamans? What are their functions and roles in the Minjung community? Most Shamans have been the victims of hard life situations. With no public channels to express their *Han*, they internalise it—and their bodies revolt. They fall sick without an identifiable medical reason. This is called *sinbyong*. The *sinbyong* (possession sickness) disappears *only when they accept the Shaman's role*. Many people believe that if possessed persons do not accept their role as a Shaman, they will die. *Sinbyong* is the unmistakable sign that one has been destined to become a Shaman.

In Korea, more than seventy per cent of Shamans are women. This statistic shows that *women are the primary transmitters and embodiment of Han* in Korean history. More specifically, poor women are the chief carriers of *Han*. They are at the bottom of the bottom in Korean society and thus may be said to embody the *Han* of the *Han*. Their possession sickness, *Sinbyong*, does not fall from the sky. Rather it comes from their everyday concrete experience of suffering. Their *Han* is caused by extreme poverty and maltreatment in a patriarchal society. When they suffer *Sinbyong*, they have:

> feelings of listlessness and later complain of many or all of the following conditions: anorexia, circulatory distresses such as extreme coldness and/or numbness of hands and feet, diarrhea, faintness, insomnia, nausea, palpitations of the heart, respiratory congestion experienced as 'heaviness of the heart' or 'tightness of the chest', acutely painful ringing in the ear, sudden fevers, and weight loss.[12]

All of this is usually accompanied by what some would call mental disorder like 'auditory and/or visual hallucinations and strange dreams'.[13]

A Korean woman anthropologist, Young Sook Kim Harvey, named the following as the most personal characteristics among Korean women Shamans:

(a) a high level of intelligence,

(b) above average capacity for creative improvisation (they were imaginative and capable of improvising verbally, behaviourally, and in the use of available resources),[1]

(c) above average verbal fluency and persuasiveness,

(d) strong goal orientation (they tended to be wilful, self-centred, self-reliant and self-directed),

(e) keen sensitivity to intuitive cues of others,

(f) calculating and manipulative inter-personal skills which enabled them to manage social situations strategically,

(g) a sharp sense of justice in terms of their own standards,

(h) an above-average repertoire of aptitudinal and/or achieved dramatic and artistic attributes, such as singing and dancing. In addition, all but one were exceptionally attractive in appearance.[14]

Shamans are strong women, 'organic intellectuals', wounded healers, exorcists, household therapists, singers, dancers, comedians, actresses—beautiful, attractive and sensual women. They are best known, however, as *priestesses* who become *mediators between the living and the dead*. In the communities of Shamanistic *Minjung*, they have no church buildings or hierarchical, clerical structures among themselves. Shamans treat people in their home or their client's home. There are no strict, orthodox texts in Shamanism.

Han-ridden ghosts are people who died in the world unjustly. Shamans call upon them during the Shamanistic ritual, *Kut*, to speak about the unjust treatment they received in this world. Then Shamans console the ghosts, negotiate with them, argue with them, and play with them. Shamans make people cry, laugh, dance, and sing through *Kut*. Shamans urge the whole community to do something for these *Han*-ridden ghosts in order to let them release their *Han* and leave this world completely with peaceful hearts. A Shaman is the spiritual centre of the community.

However, in Korean society the woman Shaman has not been treated honourably like Buddhist monks, Confucianist scholars or Christian priests and ministers. People have asked for her supernatural power to solve their problems, but they have feared her power. At the same time, they have ostracised her and her family as *the other*. Her children could not marry into so-called 'respectable' families. Traditionally, people believed that the woman Shaman exhibited a very loose sexual life. It was also believed that any man who married a Shaman would lose his masculine power and become a 'woman-like man'. A Shaman has lived an ambivalent existence. Publicly she had been powerless; but privately she is very strong.[15]

Notes

1. According to a Korean theologian, Suh Nam-dong, '*Han* is the suppressed, amassed, and condensed experience of oppression caused by mischief or misfortune so that it for a kind of "lump" in one's spirit'. See his article 'Towards a Theology of Han, in *Minjung Theology*, ed. The Commission Theological Concerns of the Christian Conference of (Singapore, Asia 1981), p. 68.

2. *Minjung* means people, specifically oppressed people.

3. 'Jiheh' is not my friend's real name. I use a pseudonym to protect her privacy.

4. Aloysius Pieris 'The Place of Non-Christian Religions and Cultures in the Evolution of Third World Theology' in *Irruption of the Third World: Challenge to Theology*, ed. Virginia Fabella and Sergio Torres (New 1983), p. 113.

5. Mercy Amba Oduyoye 'Reflections from a Third World Women's Perspective: Women's Experience and Liberation Theologies' in *Irruption of the Third World: Challenge to Theology*, p. 247.

6. Engelbert Mveng 'Third World Theology—What Theology? What Third World? Evaluation by an African Delegate' *ibid.*, p. 220.

7. General Choi Young was a real historical figure who was killed unjustly in Korean history. Pepople have venerated him as a guardian spirit in some branch of Korean Shamanism.

8. Samshin Grandmother is a kind of goddess who is in charge of fertility in Korean Shamanism.

9. Virginia Fabella and Sergio Torres (eds.) *Doing Theology in a Divided World* (New York 1985), p. xv.

10. The term 'socio-biography' of Minjung is proposed Korean Minjung theologian, Kim Yong-bok. According to Kim, the reality of Minjung can be known best not by a scientific or philosophical definition of them, but by their own life stories. For more information on 'socio-biography' of Minjung, see Kim Yong-bok 'Messiah and Minjung: Discerning Messianic Politics over against Political Messianism' in *Minjung Theology*, pp. 183–194.

11. From the preface of *Minjokwa Kut* (Nation and Kut), ed. Minjokkuthoe (Seoul 1987), p. ii.

12. Young Sook Kim Harvey 'Possession Sickness and Women Shamans in Korea' in *Unspoken Worlds: Women's Religious Lives in Non-Christian Cultures*, eds. Nancy Falk and Rita Gross (San Francisco 1980), p. 44.

13. *Ibid.*

14. Young Sook Kim Harvey *Six Korean Women: The Socialisation of Shamans* (New York 1979), pp. 235–236.

15. Laurel Kendall *Shamans, Housewives, and Other Restless Spirits* (Honolulu 1985), p. 164.

PART IV

Evolution of Third World Theological Dialogue

Sergio Torres Gonzalez

Dar-es-Salaam 1976

WHEN I was asked to contribute to this *Concilium*, I accepted the invitation with a certain hesitation, fearing that my article might lack the requisite objectively, for I have been considerably involved personally in the Ecumenical Association of Third World Theologians (ASETT) since its establishment. But I was pleased to write this piece, for ASETT has contributed very significantly to the development of theology in the Third World, helping to bring about a displacement of the social position of Western theology. The article is divided into four parts: the Background; The challenge of Dar-es-Salaam; Dar-es-Salaam in perspective; and Conclusions: *the seed bears fruit*.

1. BACKGROUND

(a) General background

The Dar-es-Salaam Conference occurred at an opportune time. The sixties and seventies were a time of awakening for the countries of the Third World, after a long period of colonial and neo-colonial exploitation and lethargy. The starting-point was the progressive independence of the African colonies and of Asia. Nevertheless, a much more important occasion was the special session of the United Nations in 1964, when the Third World countries requested a New International Economic Order; as also was the oil crisis in 1973, when the Arab countries opened up a new way for the countries producing raw materials.

In the midst of the economic, political, social and cultural awakening of the Third World, there was nevertheless the experience of a profound stirring and desire for participation and renewal in basic Christian groups. The official hierarchies of the World Council of Churches and of the Vatican supported these initiatives and opened up new opportunities and new hopes.

(b) **Specific background**

In addition to these phenomena, some meetings and conferences aroused the imagination, creativity and daring of the organisers of Dar-es-Salaam. The most important for us were the Escorial meeting,[1] and that at Ginebra and another at Detroit. At Ginebra[2] the representatives of the Black theology of the United States (James Cone and Bodipo-Malumba) and of Latin American theology (Paulo Freire and Hugo Assman) expressed their thoughts in an atmosphere of confrontation and lack of communication with European theologians. At Detroit,[3] the Latin American theologians met representatives of various theological trends from the United States, and conducted an intense and at times oppositional dialogue, and established an organisation called 'Theology in the Americas', for the development of a contextual theology in these countries, on a minority group basis.

2. THE CHALLENGE OF DAR-ES-SALAAM

The main novelty of this event was its actual occurrence. All initiatives hitherto were always made possible through the mediation of individuals or institutions in First World. It seemed too much to hope for that the Third World would find a means of coming together otherwise. Nor was there hope that it could offer any kind of original contribution. For centuries, the Third World had passively received the culture, Gospel and theology of the conquerors. Could any good come out of Nazareth? The miracle occurred at the Dar-es-Salaam meeting. At the University, in the hospitable atmosphere ensured by President Julius Nyerere, the symbol of African Socialism,[4] twenty-two theologians of the Third World changed the tradition of centuries and became the protagonists of a new age. For a moment, history seemed to have stopped—effectively, to have changed direction. The voice of the 'damned of the earth', the voice of defiance and hope, was being heard. The consumers of Western theology now dramatically challenged the old way of thinking, and proposed a new way of doing theology. With good reason, a visionary European theologian, Fr M. D. Chenu OP, called this encounter the 'Bandung of theology'. For all these reasons, Dar-es-Salaam became the symbolic starting-point of a new stage in theology. In view of the importance of this event, and since historical memory tends to become somewhat clouded, I shall try to give a reliable account of the origins, based on consultation of all the protagonists.

(a) Early steps

The first person to conceive of dialogue between Third World theologians was an African student of theology at Louvain, the Catholic theologian Oscar Bimwenyi.[5] In 1974 he told Francis Houtart, professor at the university and a great friend of the Third World, about his ideas. Houtart played a very important part in the early years of the Association.[6] The first step was the setting up of an organising committee, formed from students from a number of countries, with a co-ordinator to each continent. The co-ordinators chosen were: Oscar Bimyenyi for Africa, D. S. Amalorpoavadas[7] for Asia, and Enrique Dussel for Latin America.[8] The second step was to write to thirty theologians in three continents, asking for their opinions and ideas on the project. The first circular was composed and produced by Stan Lourdsami (Asia) and O. Bimyenyi and E. Dussel. The infrastructure was provided by SEUL (European Service of Latin American Universities) represented by Leopoldo Marmora and Meis Bockaert. The response was favourable and enthusiastic and the secretariat prepared a synthesis of these replies. In due course the dialogue was scheduled to take place at Tabora seminary in Africa.

(b) Preparation for the meeting

On 18 November 1975 there was a meeting at Louvain of A. Ngindu Mushete, who replaced Bimwenyi, Sergio Torres,[9] who replaced Enrique Dussel, and Meis Bockart, representing SEUL. Amalorpavadas was unable to attend, but expected to join the group in Nairobi, for the Assembly of the World Council of Churches, in which all of them would participate.

Nairobi was the real starting-point for the organisation of the meeting. The co-ordinators, Mushete, Torres, and Amalorpavadas, met several times and contacted various theologians who were attending the Assembly. The result was the formation of a preparatory committee and it was agreed that the first dialogue would take place in Tanzania in 1976.[10] The executive secretary designate then visited Tanzania and saw President Nyerere, who promised all possible support, and with the help of the Maryknoll sister, Marie Giblin, made the contacts needed to organise the dialogue.[11] He then flew to New York and, with the incalculably valuable help of Virginia Fabella,[12] undertook the task of sending the invitations, confirming the programme suggested by the Nairobi committee, and arranging finance. Major assistance with this last objective was forthcoming from A. Houtart, E. Castro and various European agencies, and, in the United States, the Maryknoll Fathers, E. Stockwell and various agencies as well as two support committees.

(c) The Dar-es-Salaam dialogue and the birth of ASETT

In August 1976 the meeting finally took place . . . The following theologians were present on this historic occasion: from Asia: D. S. Amalorpavadas, J. R. Chandran, Carlos Abesamis, Lynn de Silva (+), Mark Fang, Tissa Balasuriya, and Peter K. H. Lee; from Africa: A. Ngindu Mushete, Charles Nyamiti, K. A. Dickson, Edward W. Fashole-Luke, Patrick A. Kalilombe, Kofi Appiah-Kubi; from Latin America: Hugo Assman, Beatriz Melano Couch, Enrique Dussel, Gustavo Gutierrez, Gerardo Viviers (representing Jose Miguez-Bonio) and Sergio Torres. Maurice Assad came from Egypt as a representative of the Orthodox Church in Africa. Harold Sitahal (representing Idris Hamid (+)) came from the Caribbean. The US minorities were represented by C. T. Vivian, who had been with Martin Luther King. The twenty-two theologians present lived through an intensive week of historic discussion, packed with symbolism and hope. Without fully realising the significance of this meeting, the group accomplished their aim and responded to the Spirit's inspiration. In a few days they were able to get to know one another, to listen to and learn from one another, and to try to learn about the different cultures and histories of each. They experienced joy, emotion and Utopian dreams. But there were also moments of tension, disillusionment and confrontation. Beatriz M. Couch was a symbolic presence, as the only woman in this Third World patriarchal setting. There was a final expression of agreement in a document and the decision was taken to establish a permanent institution, the Ecumenical Association of Third World Theologians. A provisional constitution was composed, an executive committee was appointed[14] and a working programme for the next few years was proposed.

3. DAR-ES-SALAAM IN PERSPECTIVE

The foregoing account of events and protagonists provides the background for an analysis of their historical and theological significance.

(a) One's own space

The first major achievement of Dar-es-Salaam was to create a new space for self-expression. It was a new thing for the 'centre' to listen to the 'periphery'. Discourse and opinion are signs of power and had always been controlled by the secular and ecclesiastical powers that be. The Third World theologians were separated and without any form of common communication. The Dar-es-Salaam dialogue allowed them to meet and to establish together a space or permanent forum where their humiliated and suffering voice could be heard, with the hope that God would hear this people. Falteringly, but at the same time with assurance, an emotional note and summons appeared in the final document: 'We invite all those who practise theology in the churches to consider our suggestions and to associate with us and with all those who are struggling to build a more just world' (Final Document, no. 2).[15]

(b) The displacement of theology

The awakening of the Third World countries revealed the major contradiction between the rich and the poor nations. For Christians there was a particularly tragic note to this gulf, for it showed the division between rich and poor churches.[16] In the meeting under discussion the theologians expressed emphatically a frustration which they had experienced for some time. The frustration resulted from the realisation that the 'universal theology' of the Church was in fact a geographically localised and culturally conditioned interpretation. Theology was not universal but European. In their document the group indicated: 'The theologies of Europe and North America are still dominant in our churches; they represent a form of cultural domination. They have to be examined with regard to the special situations of those countries. They ought not to be accepted without being criticised and without being scrutinised to see if they are appropriate to the context of our countries' (Final Document, no. 31). The Dar-es-Salaam meeting was the sign of a new stage in the history of theology. It was the start of a geographical, cultural and theological displacement. Henceforth theology was removed from the 'centre' to the 'periphery'. With the development and vitality of the local churches, a beginning was made with a relevant theological discourse, an interpretation of the will of God on the basis of the experience of faith in the living Jesus Christ, present in the local communities. This displacement went further with the pluralism of the churches and of theology. The theologians of the Third World proposed a new way of thinking about salvific events. This form of reflection, on the basis of new geographical and cultural contexts, conditioned the reception of the one Gospel and affected the content of theology.

(c) An epistemological break

Nevertheless, this displacement was not only of a geographical and cultural dimensions. The theologians expressly considered a deeper gulf, and offered a fundamental and decisive affirmation which had always been present in the thought of Third World theologians. The final document says: 'Let us reject, as unimportant, an academic mode of theology which is distinct from action. We support a radical epistemological break, which is committed to making our first theological act the introduction of a critical reflection on the historical praxis of the Third World' (Final Document, no. 31).

To be sure, not all the theologians present were properly equipped to understand the consequences of this affirmation. As has been shown since then, this break is the most novel aspect of the Third World theologies and that which differentiates them from traditional academic theology. These theologies do not essentially rely on the deductive method. They arise from faith in the Lord of life; from the suffering and pain of the oppressed who are fighting for full liberation. They express a form of reflection on faith and intend greater knowledge of God, who is the object of all theologies, on the basis of liberating praxis. Furthermore, they seek to contribute to justice and to respect for human rights in all countries. This agreement on the primacy of praxis was one of the fundamental points at Dar-es-Salaam.

(d) Towards a Third World theology

The task of the Dar-es-Salaam theologians was a difficult one. It was not possible to formulate a structured theological programme on the basis of such different contexts. The unifying quest was more for an appropriate model than for a special identity. None the less, the group was able to offer some indications which were confirmed gradually. A common element, accepted by everyone, was the will to respond to the challenges offered by the state they were in as citizens of the Third World and as Christians belonging to the churches of the Third World. The context of their theology was not primarily the university or the parish but national and international suffering and injustice.

Third World theology tries to reflect on how to live the experience of God in a world divided by war, scarred by hunger and suffering, and dominated by systems of oppression and injustice. At the same time it tries to discern the signs of life and hope in the resistance of their powers to all systems of domination, and in faith in the God of life, who sustains the hope of those who are without power in the world. The theologians issue an invitation to all Christians to make theology the concrete expression of theological charity, and a way of putting into practice in our own day the parable of the Good Samaritan. As the document says: 'We issue a call to active commitment to the promotion of justice and the prevention of exploitation, of the accumulation of riches in the hands of a few people, of racism, of sexism, and of all forms of oppression, discrimination and dehumanisation' (Final document, no. 35).

(e) Development theology and theology of liberation

In Dar-es-Salaam there was no agreement on a single determined theology in the Third World. The conditions for so far-reaching and inclusive a project were absent. Nor was there an option for the theology of liberation, as might be thought on reading some sections of the final document. On the one hand, Patrick Masanja, from Tanzania, employed an analytical methodolody based on class struggle to describe the African situation.[17] The Philippines delegate, Carlos Abesamis, offered a theological presentation with a liberation emphasis.[18] Nevertheless, other delegates, like Peter Lee from Hong Kong, preferred a clear option for a theology of development.[19] In reality, there was underlying disagreement and we experienced quite deep gulfs of opinion. Some Latin American theologians seemed excessively sure of their own theology, and showed no real inclination to listen to others, and did not in fact conceal their intention and desire to put forward the Latin American theology of liberation as a universal model for the entire Third World. This development was resisted by African and Asian delegates, and there were difficult moments of tension and confrontation. Nevertheless, there is a basic need of unity and reconciliation of differences in order to confront responsibly the suffering and humiliation of the impoverished, which these theologians try variously to interpret and describe. In section 36 of the final document we find a statement of the common elements which unite them: the reality and condition of the Third World. Moreover, there is an acknowledgement of differences and of varied contexts. In particular, there is a recognition of the challenge which the non-Christian religions present for Africa and Asia. In fact, this meeting was the starting-point for a process which through divine grace has never slackened.

4. CONCLUSION: THE SEED BEARS FRUIT

The original seed would seem to have borne fruit. The tiny Dar-es-Salaam group has become a solid and established association with more than a hundred members. The Third World's best-known theologians belong to the association and are determined to ensure that it remains their own forum and a means of utilising the power of word and opinion. Dar-es-Salaam was the starting-point of this renewal and creativity. The founders deserve our respect and our gratitude. Clearly it was the Spirit of Jesus that asked us to believe and profess the truth that 'God is reconciled with his people'. In the presence and acknowledgement of the suffering people, and enlightened by the witness of our martyrs, we undertake to keep alive the flame of life and hope which was lighted at Dar-es-Salaam.

Translated by J. G. Cumming

Notes

1. Alfonso Alvarez Bolado *Fe Cristiana y Cambio Social en America Latina* (Saalamanca 1973).
2. Paulo Freire *et. al. Teologia Negra. Teologia de la Liberacion* (Salamanca 1974).
3. Sergio Torres and John Eagleson *Teologia en las Americas* (Salamanca 1980).
4. M. Traber 'Church and Socialism in Afrca. The Tanzanian Model', in *Concilium* (1977), no. 125.
5. O. K. Bimwemyi: 'A l'origine de l'association oecuménique des théologiens du Tiers Monde', in *Bulletin de Théologie Africaine*, II, 3 (1980).
6. F. Houtart helped to set up the European committee and provided a considerable part of the finance for the first three conferences.
7. Letter of D. S. Amaalorpavadas to Virginia Favella, 15 November 1966 (in the Association's archives).
8. E. Dussel 'Theologies of the Periphery and of the Centre, Encounter or Confrontation?' in *Concilium*, no. 191 (1984).
9. S. Torres, after the Detroit conference, accepted the request of the Maryknoll missionaries to prepare a dialogue between African and Latin-American theologians.
10. The committee was consisted of R. Chandran, chairman, S. Torres, executive secretary, and co-ordinating members: Mushete, Buthelezi, Dussel, Miguez Bonino and Amalorpavadas.
11. A preparatory comittee was set up in Tanzania, consisting of A. J. Temu, J. W. Butiku, Nyamiti, Marie Giblin and Kofi Appiah-Kubi.
12. Virginia Fabella is, in my opinion, the person who has contributed most to the vision, creativity, commitment and organisation of ASETT.
13. The North American committee was set up by L. Russell, T. Ryan, K. Canon, A. Chacon, M. Coakley, M. D'Escoto, V. Fabella, R. Harris, K. Hockin, R. Lambert, J. McCarthy, R. Powell, V. Russel, W. Smith, S. Smith, G. Thomas, C. T. Vivian and P. Walshe. The European committee was established by A. Camps, G. Casalis, M. D. Chenu, J. de Santa Ana, V. Cosmao, P. Fransten, P. Freire, A.

Gesche, F. Houtart, Pastor Klein, M. Klompe, J. B. Metz, J. Moltmann, N. Greinacher, I. M. Fraser, A. Jeanson, G. Montaron, H. Mottu and D. Sölle.
14. This committee was founded by R. T. Chandran, chairman; P. Kalilombe, vice-chairman, and executive secretary, Sergio Torres.
15. I quote from an ASETT photocopied edition, entitled: *Documentos Finales de las cuatro conferencias internacionales de ASETT*. The English version appears in *The Emergent Gospel* (New York 1978) pp. 2599–271.
16. V. Elizondo, N. Greinacher, eds. 'Tensions between Rich and Poor Churches' in *Concilium*, no. 164 (1981).
17. Patrick Masanja 'Neocolonialism and Revolution in Africa', in S. Torres and V. Fabella *The Emergent Gospel* (New York 1978) pp. 9–21.
18. Carlos Abesamis 'Doing Theological Reflection in a Philippines Context', *ibid.* pp. 112–23.
19. Peter K. H. Lee 'Between the Old and the New', *ibid.* pp. 124–136.

Maria Clara Lucchetti Bingemer

Third World Theologies: Conversion to Others

(Reflections on the EATWOT General Assembly held in
Oaxtepec, Mexico, in December 1986)

TO CELEBRATE ten years of its progress and work, EATWOT (The
Ecumenical Association for Third World Theologians) organised a General
Assembly of its members in Oaxtepec in Mexico from 7 to 14 December
1986. The choice of Mexico as a venue was extremely fortunate and full of
significance: standing at a confluence of ancestral, colonial and modern
cultures; a crossroads between indigenous Aztec and Maya religious
experience and the cradle of Christian evangelisation of the continent of
Latin America, Mexico offers the ideal geographical environment and
intellectual climate for an exchange and meeting of all the varied currents
of theology emanating from the various regions of the Third World.

Preceded by an international meeting of women theologians, from 1 to 6
December, the Assembly was solemnly opened on the evening of 7 De-
cember, with the delegates being set the task of examining the theme:
'Common and Distinct Elements and Cross-fertilisation among Third
World Theologies.'

The attempt to make this appraisal in common did not pass off smoothly.
As the Assembly progressed, there were difficulties and conflicts, produced

by divisions and misunderstandings within our number. In the end, however, the high quality of the papers presented and the common desire to resolve the tensions so as to achieve a fruitful exchange won through, and the Assembly must be reckoned an important stage in the growth of the Association.

Dealing with the elements common to and the differences between the three continents (Africa, Asia and Latin America) and the North American minorities, and pondering and evaluating the cross-fertilisation that can result from these, the participants emerged more clearly aware of their own identity, and determined to live and develop their theological mission as a contemplative commitment, in which methodology, choice of subject-matter and systematic examination of the experience and struggles of the oppressed will combine to produce a real experience of God and proper attention to the God of others. Seeing the revelation of God shining in the faces of others, those who are different from us, we all, as theologians, felt called to conversion and to make our theology too an effective and gratuitous instrument of conversion.

1. THE COMMON ELEMENTS OF THEOLOGICAL ENDEAVOUR

The Oaxtepec meeting showed that the Christian churches of the Third World today share a common theological purpose. They are churches that reflect on their Christian faith, and on the experiences this faith produces, in a particular context, with its particular characteristics. This reflection shares common elements, which gives the theologies of the Third World an aspect of brotherly solidarity and helps them to see each other as close to one another and part of the same overall purpose.

Third World Theologies are theologies born out of a *spiritual experience*. All the churches of the Third World are demonstrating an awakening and a new appreciation of the importance of spirituality. The peoples of the Third World—basically Christian in Latin America and among the minorities in North America, pluralist in Africa and above all in Asia—are going through, against the background of their situation of oppression, a deep and rich religious experience. A theology seeking to be of service to these peoples must necessarily be a theology that starts from a meeting with God, a meeting that takes place within a situation of challenge, a situation that awakens Christians to a *contemplative commitment*.[1] In this contemplative committed endeavour, Third World theologians are re-living the paschal mystery of Jesus Christ at every moment. Their theologies are born of the suffering and humiliations of their peoples, of their painful experience of poverty, of hunger, of genocide, of death, and at the same time of their longing for dignity and liberation based on the victory already won by Jesus Christ.[2]

More specifically, they are theologies born out of a context of injustice and oppression. This is why they are organised and expressed as rebellion against domination and exercise of power. Listening to one another at Oaxtepec, the theologians there clearly felt they all came from countries under attack: on the economic, social, political, ideological and cultural fronts. This cross weighing on the shoulders of their peoples leads them to ask who the God they adore and serve is: the God of life or the golden idol[3] hidden behind the masks of racism, sexism or naked capitalism.

Because they arise in such contexts, Third World theologies are, by nature, *combative* theologies. They attempt to introduce theological discourse within the movement of peoples organising themselves for their liberation. Their theory takes account of the praxis of these peoples, which, in its turn, leans heavily on theory. Its starting-point is experiencing and describing historical reality from both analytical and intuitive standpoints, including struggles for change to the benefit of the oppressed. Our theologies recognise that the most important thing is not their theological discourse and the words they use, but the liberation that has to take place, in the process of which theology has a part to play and a specific identity. The struggle of Third World theologies is an eschatological struggle, for the coming of the Kingdom that has to come into being now, with all the sufferings involved in the fight against the anti-Kingdom, but which will not be fully manifest till the final coming of Christ. Liberation and the struggle to bring it about form the common theme and the central experience, common to them and the peoples they serve, has till now been oppression of every sort.

Third World theologies are also *ecclesial* theologies. They need to retain and maintain their common basis in the churches, despite differences among the churches, of denomination and regional and cultural expression in the various locations in which they work, of involvement in theology and the process of liberation, of response to the situations that challenge and call out to them. Third World theologians accept and proclaim their belonging to these churches, experiencing this belonging as a reference and sometimes as a challenge. But they share a common feeling that 'the Church of Christ is God's instrument for the liberation of the human spirit so as to manifest the first-fruits of the Kingdom of God.'[4] The way Third World theologians are rooted in their churches, their resolve to do theology from within the Church, in accord with the longings and aspirations of the People of God, is something they share in common, and something that marks them out as servants of these humiliated and downtrodden peoples, praying that they may, individually or collectively, become instruments of the Kingdom of God on earth.

These common elements are counter-balanced by a series of wide divergences. Bringing out these divergent points, though it produced some shocks and even battles at the Assembly, overall proved a source of great enrichment.

2. THE QUEST FOR IDENTITY THROUGH DIFFERENCES

Observing one another in this beautiful Mexican valley, the Third World theologians could see differences in their faces that reflect the diversity of the faces of their peoples. The Oaxtepec Assembly proved an excellent opportunity for reflecting on one's own identity through one's differences from others. EATWOT has always seen itself as different from the cultures and theologies of the First World, but this time it was the differences and contrasts within itself, among its own members, that came to the fore. Even the influence of colonialism has made itself felt in different ways in the various continents, and still more among the minority peoples of the United States.[5]

The contributions from *Asia* brought out particular differences from other parts, as well as aspects in common with them. With its special privilege of being the cradle of the most ancient cultures and the birthplace of all the great world religions, cultures and religions that are still alive and deeply influential on the continent, Asia provides a strong challenge to Christian theology. Besides this, the existence of so many different races, ethnic groups, tribes and—in India—castes, gives this continent a special individuality and an almost magical power of fascination. There are also some problems common to the three continents which are seen at their starkest in Asia. The one that cries out loudest is undoubtedly the domination of women, who are exploited in the home, at work, in social life, devalued as human beings to an extreme degree.

In view of this complex panorama, Asia presents challenges not found to the same degree on the other continents, such as how the Judeo-Christian revelation should enter into dialogue with the ancient religions of the East. How are the basic truths of revelation—the mystery of the incarnation, the Holy Trinity, the eschatological destiny of humankind—to be regarded within the framework of Eastern philosophies, of the sacred books of India and China? And how, on the other hand, do we, in dialogue with non-Christian religions, both teach and learn from them when dealing with concepts so basic and dear to Third World Christian theology as the integral liberation of human beings, the development of social justice, and so on?

Africa, besides the elements it shares with the other continents, also has its own characteristics, giving the oppression its peoples suffer from its own identity. This identity, paradoxically, appears as a threat to the identity of the continent, which suffers from excessive linguistic fragmentation, founded on the fragmentation brought about by colonisation: French-, English-, Portuguese- and Arabic-speaking Africa is still crushed and subjugated by these outside cultures telling it what it should say and think. Besides this, Africa is the only continent of the planet which still suffers, in the apartheid regime of South Africa, from the worst racist scandal in the history of humanity, exceeding even Nazism and blind anti-Semitism in its horror and tyranny.[6]

On the basis of these exceptional factors, African speakers at Oaxtepec developed the concept of *anthropological poverty*. This means more than poverty on the material level; it seeks to give an account of the exploitation and slavery to which the black peoples were subjected, and of the way in which they themselves have interiorised the patterns, values and models of the slave-owning powers. In the face of this anthropological poverty, Western Christendom is called to pronounce a humble '*mea culpa*', confessing its sin of complicity in European colonisation and of omission in failing to denounce the abuses of power that took place on the continent. This theme of anthropological poverty, dear and proper to Africa and distinguishing it from the other Third World continents, branches out into two main channels: that of the *inculturation* of Christianity, which must take on the particular forms of the native cultural matrices if it is to live and proclaim the gospel and the apostolic tradition; and that of *liberation* on the social, economic and cultural levels as the means of overcoming the pervasive anthropological poverty. The centrality of culture in African concern is steering the theology being developed there toward a humanism based on solidarity, ancestor worship, a mystique of life that includes the dead, thereby bringing the rites and customs and the whole rich panoply of African culture within a theological framework.

Latin America generally continues its theological development of the theme of social, economic and political liberation. The Christian churches of the continent that produced the list of faces taken by poverty, in the Puebla Final Document—the faces of young children, of young people, of the indigenous peoples, the peasants, labourers, the underemployed and unemployed, marginalised and overcrowded urban dwellers, old people[7]— are gradually opening out the fan of this vision of the poor as the privileged recipients of theology and the agents of the struggle for their rights, their dignity, their liberation. Latin American theological thought is incorporating a mass of pedagogical reflection: on the means of working with the people in terms of popular education, community meetings, Bible study groups. The theology produced on the continent has, in turn, moved out from academic circles into the streets, informal discussions, the press and the communications media.

Latin America is also witnessing the emergence of three large groups, previously marginalised and now coming forward to challenge the Christian churches and their theology in a way that is bound to bring deep questioning and change. They are: first, the *blacks*, who previously organised themselves in separate councils and brotherhoods, but are now looking to find their own place within the main body of the Church, in the fields of ministry, liturgy and theology itself; then, the *Amerindians*, who are regaining their own tradition and dignity in the sphere of the churches, interlinking religious renewal with the struggle for the indigenous cause, the recognition of their tribal lands, the preservation of their culture; finally, *women*, who are rising up and making a new voice heard, a voice different in tone and content, producing a new way of doing theology.

The North American minorities—Indians, blacks and hispanics—are the oppressed and discriminated-against presence of the Third World in the heart of the most typical country of the First: the United States. Poor— trying to carve out a place in a society that has no room for them—these North American minorities are now daring to try and create something new, expressed in Black theology,[8] in the richness of the religious experience of the hispanic peoples, and now emerging as a significant presence in the Association of Third World Theologians.

3. CROSS-FERTILISATION

The first piece of cross-fertilisation that can be reported concerned the question of methodology. We found that it is in the struggle for fuller life that we meet the God of life and so discover our method of doing theology. Our theologies are not great principles to be applied to reality, but an orientation to clarify our commitment and practice, to establish new relationships and a new life style.

Among the great themes of theology, Christology is one that is greatly enriched by the cross-fertilisation brought about by the meeting of Third World theologies. The continent of Asia above all teaches us how to safeguard the originality of Jesus over against other forms of manifestation of the Word of God, how to unite the Jesus of history and the cosmic Christ, in a richly pneumatic Christology and a cosmo-theandric vision of reality.

Cross-fertilisation also took place on the level of our understanding of our mission as *Church*. In Oaxtepec, the different continents and religions were able to question one another on the quality and relevance of their ecclesial mission of evangelisation, and on their churches' understanding of themselves as disciples among disciples, seeking a greater and better participation of God's truth.

4. CONCLUSION: CONVERSION TO OTHERS

The great lesson that came from this Assembly was the need for us, as an Association, to be activated ever more deeply and persistently by a profound movement of conversion to others. Despite the moments of tension and polarisation we experienced, the final outcome of the Assembly was our discovery of the possibility of moving beyond these differences and reaffirming reconciliation in truth and love.

The work of Third World theologians is directed toward a global view of humanity. Challenged by the differences we found among ourselves, we have come out of this Assembly more open and better disposed to stimulate dialogue and exchange, to allow ourselves to be reached and influenced by difference and otherness. In this way we—speaking from the powerlessness and fragility of the situation of the Third World—feel more capable of daring to devise and create something new.

May the Creator Spirit, who at the dawn of time hovered over original chaos and drew creation from it, come down on and act in the work of these theologians, allowing them to move in the direction of conversion to others and experience of the God of others, to take on together their enriching differences and—in the five years till the next General Assembly of their Association—produce a new theology for the whole world.

Translated by Paul Burns

Notes

1. See what L. Boff says on this subject of 'committed contemplation', in 'A teologia do Terceiro mundo' *REB* 49 (1986) p. 848: '. . . a contemplation that mobilises for transforming action and . . . an action that requires contemplation . . .'

2. See S. Rayan *Commonalities, Differences and Cross-fertilisation among Third World Theologians*, A Document of the Seventh International Conference of the Ecumenical Association of Third World Theologians (EATWOT), Oaxtepec, Mexico, 7–14 December 1986, p. 3.

3. Rayan, *op. cit.* p. 3.

4. *Ibid.*

5. For example, Latin America is the most Westernised continent and serves to show how complex the phenomenon of Western European Christianity is.

6. See R. Mveng *Rapport sur l'Afrique*, p. 2.

7. *Puebla: Conclusions* (Washington, DC, and Slough 1980), nn. 31–39.

8. See J. Cone *A Black Theology of Liberation* (Maryknoll, NY ²1987).

CONCLUSION

Samuel Rayan

Third World Theology: Where Do We Go From Here?

1. IT'S A LONG ROAD TO FREEDOM

THE 'HERE' in that question represents a point where Third World theology (TWT) now stands. It includes the present shape of that theology with its achievements, struggles and frustrations as well as memories of its evolutionary history. Where do we go from that point of arrival? The question could be the voice of perplexity or of despair. It could mean we have come to a crossroads; in what direction is our next step to be? We have landed on uncharted, trackless theological territory; how do we proceed blazing a trail? Or, more radically, the question could mean we have reached an impasse; we have exhausted our resources and possibilities; we have no more dreams and visions; and blocking our path stands an angel with a flaming sword. Does TWT, then, have a future?

Even if there were no future for it, still the little this theological movement has accomplished must be recognised as significant. Its sojourn, however brief, is already leaving its mark on the universe of theologies. The world of theological reflection cannot but be different for the birth of TWT. This theological movement springs from suffering and humiliation born of poverty on the one hand and from people's will to dignity and resistance to oppression on the other. Its origin is in people's experience of misery and death. It is protest against domination no less than striving for justice and liberation. The story of TWT is the story of liberational praxis, the struggles of the dispossessed and the wretched of the earth to win back their right to life and creative existence. It is the story of the price paid in terms of people's blood and life in their long combat for humanity and dignity.

Praxis is pregnant with theory. The praxis of liberation carries within it a liberating theology. A service of theological midwifery could help bring the baby to birth. Many a significant liberational conflict has been reflected on by the struggling people themselves, and its deepest meaning spelt out. The result of one such endeavour is the liberation theology we call Exodus (chapters 1–15). The main thought-stream in the rest of the Bible consists of further reflection by a Third World people on this and subsequent experiences of oppression, struggle and liberation. The Indian myths of Divine Descents (*avataara*) have each a distinct liberational thrust. Many an ancient (*puraana*) story is in all probability a people's story of resistance to oppression. The liberational dimensions of Buddhism deserves careful study. It is an active liberation spirituality that the Bhagavad-Gita expounds in the context of armed resistance to enthroned might and fraud. In the sixteenth century Carribean, Bartolome de las Casas sketched a TWT in his critical rejection of the religion of European conquerors, gold-grabbers and genocides as well as in his description of (original) Americans as other than raw material for evangelisation, and as 'the scourged Christ of the Indies'.

Third World theology continued its journey through widespread Afro-American struggle against enslavement; through the two (1871 and 1885) metis' rebellions in Canada led by Louis Riel;[1] through resistance to British penetration of the Sudan, led by the religious-military movement of the Mahdis of when eleven thousand were gunned down by the British in one afternoon; and further through the 'shini (new) lama' movement at the turn of the century in Inner Mongolia, led by a lay priest of Buddhism to defend the Mongol herdsmen against land take-overs by Han who was put under pressure by British policies in South China and the infamous opium wars. The journey has continued through the numberless peasant revolts in colonised India and elsewhere, through the peasant wars of this century, and through the struggles for national independence which overthrew militant colonialism in our days.[2] Gandhiji saw his work as fight for the freedom of Britain in the first place and of India too. Both had become alienated through loss of identity and authenticity: India was degraded to slavehood while Britain had decayed into becoming slave-master and international bully.

Since 1960 formal critical reflection has been brought to bear on various kinds of oppression, giving rise to several powerful currents of liberation and Third World theologies. These articulate the struggles of ethnic groups against racist oppression; of women against sexist oppression and patriarchy; of Africans against cultural oppression which they have named anthropological pauperisation—a European attempt at total negation and complete obliteration of African humanity; and of all the ex-colonies against socio-economic and political oppression, littered by imperialist policies, old and new, of systematic underdevelopment, exploitation and plunder. Since 1976 various theological currents and concerns have come together to form the Ecumenical Association of Third World Theologians (EATWOT) which has to date held seven international conferences and several continental and regional consultations and colloquia. TWT is part of people's life—a way of being believers and human beings who think and search; an atmosphere of critical reflection which people shape and re-shape as they build their history. There exists also considerable literary output in TWT in several languages and translations. That is where the long road to freedom has brought us, where TWT stands today. Before we consider questions of any further possible/impossible journey, we shall do well to take stock of what we have in hand to our credit as we stand here.

2. WHAT HAVE WE ACHIEVED?

We believe that our greatest gain is the articulation of our methodology. We refuse the classical way of starting from Church teaching or Bible, deducing theological conclusions and applying them to historical reality. We start rather from concrete social reality and a preferential option for the down-trodden and commitment to their liberation. We read social reality—as also the Bible and history—from below, from the perspective of the poor, through their tears and wounds, through the struggles and hopes of the oppressed. Committed liberational praxis to effect real change in human relations in the direction of greater equality and justice is the first act. Theology follows as fruit of critical reflection on socially transformative praxis. Change occurring or brought about ceaselessly in persons and societal realities dictates continuing change in our interpretation of the Bible and of Church teaching. To quote J. L. Segundo: '. . . each new reality obliges us to interpret the Word of God afresh, to change reality accordingly, and then to go back and re-interpret the Word of God again, and so on.'[3]

Another significant step has been the organising of EATWOT. Its purpose is to enable Third World situations on all the continents to reflect and move together in developing TWT; in witnessing to the New Humanity disclosed in Christ through shared struggles for a New Order; and in interpreting the Gospel as the power of God enabling the poor to sustained combat. The Association has proved to be a fruitful forum of exchange, support, mutual challenge, collaboration and cross-fertilisation of minds and ideas. For over ten years now, 'we have remained united across tensions and conflicts, and have come to respect each other in each other's otherness, to see what is different as an enrichment for all, and to hold our diversities within a comprehensive commitment to the liberation of the people from every form of oppression'.[4]

Mention must be made of the discovery of the poor, with liberated consciousness as the subject of theology. Through political struggles the poor become theological actors. Their faith in God is becoming a central element in their political awakening and social mobilisation. It is a faith bound up with the culture of the rural poor and the wisdom of workers, both forged and mellowed in the crucible of suffering. In the area of politics the poor are seeking to create something new—with less police and prison and more space for all to participate. It is in terms of solidarity with the poor in their struggles, and in terms of reading reality and scriptures from the viewpoint of the poor that Third World theologians define themselves. We have learned to join Jesus in giving thanks to God for giving the New Order and its Gospel to little ones, and not to the learned and the powerful.'The struggles of the poor are seen as a critical instrument for the renewal of theological reflection and spiritual life'.[5]

Our intercontinental contacts and criticisms have led us to a new sense and fresh valuation of all the great religions of the world with their spiritual traditions, saints and holy scriptures; as also of non-scriptural primal religions which are more ancient, supple and profoundly influential; and of popular religiosity with its devotions and observances which we once tended to ignore as childish or criticise as superstitious. In numerous instances traditional religions have been a source of strength and inspiration for people in their resistance to colonial aggression and imperial domination. They have thus been God's allies in defending life and dignity against an enslaving and oppressive Christianity. The encounter with peoples' religions and spiritualities has been an experience of import, as unsettling as it was health giving.

Our methodology has restored us to the ancient unity of theology and spirituality, which had flourished before theology moved out of the warmth of (monastic) piety into the cold halls of academic rationality. 'Theology is spiritual activity, a function of our faith in Christ, interior to our faith-union in God. Worship opens us up to the call of the Spirit who pervades history and enables the poor'. By the same token we have come to discover the close relatedness of 'spirituality and politics, contemplation and commitment, our understanding of God and the conflictual process of becoming human'. The Spirit of the Lord and freedom go together. The Spirit is partner in all history's struggles for authentic freedom and love, however fragmentary. 'The spirituality which is at the source of TWT consists in a passionate commitment to God's Reign on Earth, and therefore to the Earth and to its liberation and transformation. It is a spirituality which challenges the poor to throw off their yoke and be free'.[6]

Implied in the affirmation of the unity of spirituality and theology is the cognate affirmation of a dialectical relationship between orthopraxis and orthodoxy. All religions have a concern for truth and doctrine. But the truth is in life and praxis rather than in words with little rooting in deeds. It is not orthodoxy or dogmas that religions worry about. Their accents fall on orthopraxis, on spiritual, moral and social attitudes and involvements. The religious approach to reality as mystery is naturally suspicious of 'clear and distinct' definitions and dogmas as too narrow, partial and superficial expressions of reality.[7] Truth is not something that can be known and spoken independently of its realisation in life. 'Thus truth and fidelity are intimately united in the Bible . . . God is truthful because he does what he promises . . . Biblical truth is characterised by the fact that it is projected into history . . . Theology then is an understanding of this faith that is accepted and lived out.'[8] We are convinced that it is idle to concentrate on formulating 'truths' while doing next to nothing to better the world. In the absence of orthopraxis, orthodoxy would lack a mother to be born from. A. Pieris, referring to Amilcar Cabral, Patrice Lumumba, Nkruma and Ho Chi Minh, reminds us that these men 'wrote little and transmitted much to posterity through their praxis, which therefore serves as a *locus theologicus* for those groping for a liberation theology of religions and cultures'.[9]

Third World theology goes with martyrdom. This is true of many a scene in Central and South America. It is true of South Africa and places like South Korea, Singapore, Malaysia, and US dominated Philippines. Doing theology and interpreting God's Word for life in today's history has become risky. Tens of thousands of people, lay and religious, priests and bishops included, have disappeared, been exiled, tortured and killed for speaking the Word and standing with God on the side of the oppressed. This is not new. Leonardo Boff recounts stories of martyrs from the beginning of European conquest and colonisation of the Americas to our own times.[10] In countries called 'catholic', whose leaders attend Mass and venerate the Virgin, Christians who act according to their faith are abducted, imprisoned, tortured, raped, used as forced labour, mutilated, crushed to death, gunned down in considerable numbers. 'The shame of our times', indeed![11] Small segments of this contemporary martyrology has been made available.[12] These tell of a few of those who in Latin America in our times have sacrificed their lives in the struggle for the Gospel and justice. Their martyrdom bears witness to a theology which, says, Karl Rahner, 'knows well how to shoulder responsibility for the poor and the needy'. An authentic theology, therefore, which has 'a footing at a spot from which leads a path that goes all the way to the end—when persons sacrifice their lives for their fellows.'[13]

The existence of a distinct TWT with a different methodology marks the definitive admission of theological pluralism and the abolition of the West's monopoly in theology. A dozen years ago Cardinal Villot, speaking in Abidjan, scoffed at the idea of an African theology since theology could only be one, namely catholic; that is, in fact, European. John Paul II speaking to bishops of Zaire in 1983, warned them of the danger of 'allowing the growth of a philosophy and a theology of "Africanism" that would be exclusively of native origin and lacking any real or profound connection with Christ.' To avoid the risk of becoming closed in on oneself, the Pope prescribed 'sound collaboration with the centres of study in other countries'—meaning, of course, Western countries.[14] The assumption is that Western, or European, centres of studies are immune to such risks and dangers even when for centuries they sought no collaboration with centres of studies 'in other countries', but sought rather to impose their own native philosophies and theologies on the rest of the world. Theology has now shaken free of eurocentric cultural shackles and is at liberty to speak in a variety of idioms and accents, and to highlight essential dimensions of the Gospel which for long have been suppressed or distorted by dominant socio-ecclesiastical ideologies and interests.

A last point worth noting is that in TWT the voiceless have found a voice. They have spoken out and won a hearing. They have been heard both by friend and foe. Many friends in the First World have given us support, begun to work out analogous methodologies for their contexts, translated our works into First World languages, and published introductory surveys and critical studies of TWT.[15] TWT has also been taken hostile note of in high political circles. The US government was the first to take it seriously. Latin American oligarchs and military regimes followed suit. So did the Vatican, though not without hesitancy and ambiguity. Caricature, calumny and police action as well as subtly manipulated isolation are some of the weapons used against TWT till they are replaced, which is soon enough, with scientific torture and the machine gun. Peter Hebblethwaite, writing about Fernando Cardenal, notes that 'in Nicaragua there is concern at the way Cardinal Ratzinger's condemnation of liberation theology can be linked with President Reagan's Santa Fe speech against liberation theology—the religious and the political going hand in hand'.[16] It all means that TWT cannot be ignored. It is a ferment with historical consequences which are welcomed or feared according to one's class position, political ideology or understanding of the faith. At any rate, the Christian community cannot ignore TWT. 'Unless the Christian Church is to become no more than a Society for the Preservation of the Privileged and the Prosperous, we cannot ignore liberation theologies. They are the Church's harbingers of a most profound expression of agony and hope for the peoples of the Third World.'[17]

3. AGONY AND HOPE

If TWT is an expression of agony and hope for Third World people, it cannot be wholly futureless. If we have come to some crossroads or some trackless waste, it is up to us to orient ourselves and get to work. The criteria which will govern our choices are present indeed in our methodology and in the treks we have covered. The touchstone always is ever deeper humanisation through liberation and responsibility, justice, fellowship and participation.

The situation of pauperisation and oppression continues and in some places continue to worsen. The process of economic underdevelopment, dependency and exploitation, introduced by colonial powers, goes on, and is complicated by the presence in our midst of imperialism's local allies, colonised minds, growth models, thought patterns, and the debt trap. The result is the appalling poverty and misery of the masses of the Third World alongside abominable opulence and luxury of a small elite group. Scandalous social gaps and distortion of our continents is also carried on through the media, the educational system and the effective blocking of the emergence of indigenous technologies. Loss of our culture is the loss of our soul, of our identity, and of our key to survival. Racism is a distinct force of oppression, insolently rampant in South Africa and the US and several First World countries as well as in Third World lands under other names and guises. The political realities of the Third World, sequel to the system of economics, education and administration introduced by colonialism, operate today in terms of disunity and bloody strife, heavy militarisation, corruption and venality in high places, and the stepping up of repression as people grow restless and resistance mounts. For the masses, even economic development means intensified exploitation.[18] J. L. Segundo notes that 'according to recent information, in one single region of Brazil, in the last five years, ten million people died of malnutrition'.[19] People's resistance to militarism, dictatorships and imposed misery is perhaps the most significant aspect of Third World reality today. The fundamental common factor in all our continents is people in search of dignity, meaning and full humanity.

That means the work will continue. As long as people refuse to give up their quest for life or to suspend their liberation struggles TWT is in the making, and is crying out for articulation.

4. WHERE DO WE GO?

From now on our theological endeavour will aim at defining a *total human perspective*. The need is to overcome dichotomies and develop a comprehensive vision of the future from the memory of which we can live and hope and risk life for the other, the oppressed and the broken. Liberation remains the common theme and central concern. But that calls for the liberation of our theology from narrow sectarian concepts. We must come to an appreciation of revelation and grace on the basis of the Spirit and in terms of history and the cosmos, in terms of the sense of mystery and the memory of the divine that constitutes the human heart. Our theology will then work with an understanding of faith as collaboration in God's best wishes for our world, collaboration with God active in the totality of world history no less than in our particular histories. Oppression will then be seen as practice of godlessness, as apostasy from the faith. And the process of liberation will be experienced as a joint venture in which God and the people are partners.

The main obstacle to faith-collaboration in God's dreams for our history must be discerned in the dominant global socio-economic system, for the success of which, Lord Keynes instructs us, religion's gentle and generous ideals must be set aside in favour of the god of private profit accumulation. It is time for the Gospel's exclusive alternative, God *or* Mammon, to be re-accented in all its starkness. A thoroughgoing theological criticism of capitalism and its ideologies and cultural components is an imperative. There we shall locate the chief source of dehumanising disparities and alienating relationships as well as the historical cause of the misery of the masses and of widespread poverty in the midst of actual and potential plenty. The work begun in such reflections as F. Hinkelammert's *Ideological Weapons of Death* must be carried further. Is it really possible to reconcile New Testament emphasis on solidarity, sharing, sacrifice, co-operation and mutuality with capitalism's basic principles of production and profit? Or with the actual experience of five or more centuries of its history?

Two points call for special attention. One is the refusal of the First World to confess responsibility for the pauperisation, mess and misery now plaguing the Third World. The responsibility must be historically and theologically determined and squarely laid where it belongs. The light of that truth is necessary to nail the lies now being passed around and to defuse the confusion of analyses now being used to prevent change. Locate the responsibility in the colonial history of the West and its neo-colonial policies of today. The second point has to do with the debt weighing upon most Third World peoples. It is one of capitalism's most successful traps. It eats fatally into all our national earnings and into all our hopes of freedom and growth. We are bound or free 'to raise the moral and theological question of repayment and restitution. In a straightforward and honest historical and ethical view of things, the real question is, *Who indeed owes what to whom?* The vast sums of money in question are but a small fraction of the enormous wealth violently transferred from the Third World to the West and continues to be transferred through a variety of colonial and neo-colonial economic and political mechanisms. It is a task of TWT to go into this matter with competence, clarity and courage as Tissa Balasuriya once did in the case of Sri Lankan Tea.'[20]

To a clear, sociologically and theologically well argued rejection of feudal-capitalist systems should respond a commitment to a viable and human form of socialism. This is in the inmost logic of Third World theology's commitment to the poor and to the new order of God, marked by justice, freedom and fellowship as well as the sharing of life's resources as symbolised in our Eucharistic celebrations. A prophetic criticism of historical socialism, its blind spots, weaknesses and failures and its tendency to become non-dialectical and dogmatic is surely in order. That critique is meant to contribute towards appreciating the appearance of socialism and its however modest historical achievements as a step forward in the history of humanisation, and as a seed of life full of promise for the future.

We are the Church, the Body of Christ in contemporary history. We *are* it in the measure in which we *become* it by living out the commitment of Jesus to God's new order of liberating the downtrodden and lifting up the lowly so that 'there may be equality'. It is therefore incumbent on us to engage in a shared critique our ourselves as Church in order to detect and eliminate the *unchurch* which keeps infiltrating into the Body of Christ.' This criticism will be part of love's labour to become the Church and rebirth it anew in every age. The work of rebuilding, already under way in the shape and life of base Christian communities and in the meditations of Third World thinkers,[21] has to be pursued with gladness and thoroughness. Our ecclesial self-criticism will bear on such alien elements as class division and class interests operative in the Body of the Church; contradictory understanding of the faith within the Church; the ideological manipulation of faith which enables rich Christians calmly to persecute and kill poor Christians; the seemingly accepted divorce between war and flesh, orthodoxy and orthopraxis; and in particular the Church's frenzied anticommunism used by the rich and the dictators to kill by the thousand. As an institution we have much to repent of and ask pardon for: from Jews and Muslims and Hindus; from the poor of the world; from native Americans, Africans and Asians, from women in Church and society. As Church we shall explore the conditions under which the Our Father can be meaningfully said among us and the Eucharistic Bread broken. The crucial question is, What makes the Church Christian? And what is the relation between people's struggles for liberation and the *becoming* of the Church? Reflection is urgent on the entire ecclesial community's authority of faith to bear witness, and its need to learn from the magisterium of history and of humankind and of the many spiritual traditions and religious visions God has nursed and guided down the centuries in so many places.

It is not enough that women be adequately represented in assemblies of Third World theologians. Neither would it do to say that because women are there men do theology in a deeper way. Women have their own way of sensing the meaning of the faith and pursuing theological reflection. Women's and men's theologies should not be left to run parallel, and never meet. Should we not look for a whole new style of doing theology, and of doing it together? A fruitful search in that direction is only possible within the wider horizons of the entire issue of womanhood. The focus of this major issue 'moves beyond the question of the equality of rights . . . to the question of meaning and significance of that equality'. In addition to the reality of women and her rights, it includes her relationship to man and their joint relationship to life. But now 'both man and woman go their divided ways, each becoming inwardly estranged from the life of the other and each in that estrangement losing contact with life'.[22] Women are persons; they are life-source both physically and psychologically; they are basic educators, and real economists in the most radical sense of the word. Women are the first communicators of cultures, values and the faith. They are the first, indispensable, God-appointed magisterium. Women are inspirers and supporters of the best in man, and not only of the worst. These are facts. If the Bible and the Church contradict them, the Bible and the Church need help to correct and reinterpret themselves truthfully.

A whole world of theological work remains to be done in relation to the religions of the world. Their providential significance; the role they have played and still play in giving meaning and direction to hundreds of millions of human beings for far longer stretches of time than biblical religions have been doing; their meaning as mediation of revelation, grace and salvation; the inspired character of their scriptures—are all weighty problems for TWT to explore in close collaboration and dialogue with adherents of these religions and against the backdrop of our faith about their origin in the heart of a God-oriented and graced history. The religions are there are mediations of God's Word and life to one another, as mutual invitation to transcendence and as symbols of the riches of the incomprehensible, unnameable mystery. How then do religions become ambiguous, and fall prey to manipulative ideologies, and turn into opium of the people, and tools of oppression, fragmentation and death? At the moment we lack a methodology to speak of world religions. Approaching every religion from the perspective of the Bible alone has its problems.

The contours of a Third World Christology are already clear. Our take-off point is not ontology but history. Jesus lived on this earth, a human being among humans, like us in all things except that he was never closed to reality but wholly open to nature, people and God. He grew in love and became it ever more completely and purely. He identified with the poor and was in solidarity with the oppressed—and discerned the cause of the downtrodden as God's cause in history. Solidarity with the oppressed, solidarity with God—a love that transformed him into itself and is kin to what is deepest and most alive in God. The conclusion is that what is done to the poor and the lowly is done to Jesus—is done to God. That is the orientation of Third World Christology. Four US women were abducted by security forces in San Salvador and were killed and buried in a cow pasture. Of them Jon Sobrino said: 'Maura, Ita, Dorothy and Jean are Christ dead today. But they are also the risen Christ who keeps alive the hope of liberation'. Salvation comes from Jesus. Salvation comes through Mary. It comes through all women and men who love truth and love people to the extent of giving their own life.[23] Jesus suffers now, is scourged and crucified now, in Catholic countries, in prisons and slums and mines and plantations. We must rediscover the real presence of Christ in the poor and the continuation of his liberating death in the oppressed. This real presence should not be muted or obscured with loose language about the Eucharist. The bread is his Body because first this suffering community is his body, his vicar on earth, his priestly mediation between heaven and the earth. Pieris has pointed out that devotion to the Sacred Heart does not consist in becoming pathological about 'reparation' for damage done to that heart. The point is that there does exist a reality in Christ capable of suffering damage and therefore reparable. Liberation theology puts us in touch with such a Christ whose bleeding heart demands brave deeds of love;—a Christ hungry, thirsty, naked, sick, homeless and fettered by social chains (Mt. 25:31–46) . . . Christ who is a threat to Herod's security and therefore hunted out by him (Mt. 2:13–15); . . . Christ tortured by the army (Mt. 27.30) . . . Christ the victim of priestly fanaticism and political opportunism (Mt. 27:15–26).[24] We have no Christology without the numberless crosses of history mediating God's love, and without the resistance of the oppressed presaging the resurrection which God is already operating in our midst. Where is the Christ? And where today is God present and active to befriend the world to himself?

We shall tell more stories, tell all the stories, of loving and suffering people. We shall tell the stories of the struggles of peoples in our respective histories. The struggles of Dalits and Untouchables; of native Americans and Africans, of slaves and bonded labourers, of patriots, freedom fighters, social reformers and risk-takers. Tell the stories and let revelation in significant events shine forth. We have yet to reflect and spell out the theology of our stories and our national struggles for independence, and of the great revolutions of China, Cuba, Zimbabwe, Vietnam, Angola, Nicaragua.

When we, Third World people, come together to do theology and share riskful commitments, we shall no longer be an exclusive club of professionals and academicians, but brothers and sisters in the liberational struggles of peasants, workers, the poor, the illiterate, the young, the voiceless. We shall make sure that some of these are there with us; that they have ample opportunities to express themselves in their own way; and that what they share will be substantial ingredients in the theological outcome. This is a demand of our methodology and our conviction that the Gospel is addressed to the poor; and that the oppressed—become awake—are the subject of theology.

It is likely that the greater the part played by the poor in insighting and articulating the meaning of the faith for today, the lesser will be the use of sophisticated scientific mediations and erudite language. Should not theology be expressed more and more in art forms—in dance and drama, in pictures and lines, in carving and sculptures? It should become embodied above all in new and beautiful relationships, in deeds of love, and finally in the new social order itself, in the beauty and shape of the just and free and equal fellowship of God's children and Christ's friends?

We conclude with a story:

'Nearly twenty years ago an Irish artist and I were invited to the old Maynooth to speak to the students on the subject of Sacred Art. . . . I rose to speak, stumbled longwindedly through my set piece and sat down, damned by faint applause.

'My friend and fellow artist got to his feet, then, and with covert and evil smile in my direction, produced from the voluminous folds of his overcoat a piece of his own sculpture. Placing it reverently on the table before him, he intoned (there is no other word for it) the memorable statement, "This is what I have to say".' He sat down, of course, to tumultuous applause.

'He was right. It is true; deepest things, the trust, the things that seem to matter . . . the visual artist can go nowhere near saying rightly in words.'[25]

Notes

1. See Douglas Daniels 'Louis Riel and Liberation Theology' in *The Ecumenist*, 25/3 (1987) pp. 33–36.
2. A. R. Desai *Peasant Struggles in India*; Eric Wolf *Peasant Wars of the Twentieth Century* (1969).
3. L. J. Segundo *The Liberation of Theology* (1976) p. 8.
4. S. Rayan *A Splash of Colours* (MSS).
5. *ibid.*
6. *ibid.*
7. See D. S. Amalorpavadass *The Church as a Community of Faith in the Indian context*. FABC paper 30 (1982) p. 14.
8. Raul Vidales 'Methodological Issues in Liberation Theology', in Gibellini (ed): *Frontiers in Theology* pp. 38–39.
9. A Pieris 'The Place of Non-Christian Religions and Cultures in the Evolution of Third World theology', in *CTC Bulletin* 3/2 (August 1982) p. 46.
10. L Boff *Passion of Christ: Passion of the World* (1987) pp. 118–121.
11. The phrase is Cardinal J. Ratzinger's. See his 1984 'Instruction on certain aspects of Liberation Theology'.
12. See for instance M. Lange and R. Iblacker *Witnesses of Hope. The persecution of Christians in Latin American* (1981). T. Cabestrero *Blood of the Innocent. Victims of Contras' War in Nicaragua* (1985). Fernando Bermudez *Death and Resurrection in Guatemala* (1986).
13. K. Rahner *Forward to Witnesses Hope* p. xiii and xv.
14. See Osservatore Romano, 1 August 1983.
15. See R. McAfee Brown *Theology in a New Key* (1978); Alfred T. Hennelley *Theologies in conflict, The Challenge of J. L. Segundo* (1979); T. Witvliet *A Place in the Sun. Liberation Theologies in the Third World* (1985); D. W. Ferm *Third World Liberation Theology. An Introductory Survey* (1986); L. L. Wostyn *Exodus Towards the Kingdom. A Survey of Latin American Liberation Theology* (1986); Roger Haight *An Alternative Vision* (1985).
16. P. Hebblethwaite 'Pastor in Revolution' in *The Tablet*, 4 August 1984.
17. W. K. McElaveny *Good News is Bad News is Good News* (1980) p. 3.
18. See *Witnesses to Hope*, p. 19.
19. J. L. Segundo *Theology and the Church* (1985) p. 166.
20. S. Rayan *A Splash of Colours* (MSS).
21. See L. Boff: *Church: Charism and Power. Liberation Theology and the Institution Church* (1985) and *Ecclesiogenesis. The Basic Communities Reinvent the Church* (1986); A. Barreiro *Basic Ecclesial Communities. The Evangelisastion of the Poor* (1976); J. Comblin *The Church and National Security State* (1979); E. Dussel *A History of the Church in Latin America* (1981); J. Sobrino: *The True Church and the Poor* (1984).

22. Josephine Newman 'The Women's Movement in the Church', in *Doctrine and Life* March 1984.

23. Quoted by P. Jacobsen in *Witnesses of Hope*, p. 153.

24. A. Pieries 'Spirituality in Liberational Perspective', in *East Asian Pastoral Review* 2 April (1983) p. 150.

25. Ray Carrol 'The Image of Christ And An Apologia for the Artist', in *The Furrow*, August, 1981.

Contributors

MARIA CLARA LUCCHETTI BINGEMER is married with three sons. She teaches Systematic Theology at the Pontifical Catholic University of Rio de Janeiro, the St Ursula University and the Franciscan Institute in Petropolis. She is working on a doctoral thesis for the Gregorianum in Rome. Her most recent works include *Escatologia Cristã* (with João Libânio) and *Maria, mãe de Deus e Mãe dos Pobres* (with Ivone Gebara) of which an English translation is in progress, to be published in 1989 as *Mary, Mother of God and Mother of the Poor.*

LEONARDO BOFF was born in Brazil in 1938 and ordained priest in the Franciscan Order in 1964. He studied in Curitiba, Petrópolis. He is also co-editor of *Concilium* and national adviser to the base Church communities. His many books on various aspects of liberation theology include *Jesus Christ Liberator, Church: Charism and Power* (1984), which earned him the censure of the former Holy Office, *Trinity and Society* (1988) and *Passion of Christ: Passion of the World.*

CHUNG HYUN-KYUNG was born in Korea in 1956. She graduated from Ewha Women's University in Seoul and came to the USA and completed the MDiv at the School of Theology at Claremont, California. Before coming to Union Theological Seminary in New York for her doctorate, she attended the Women's Theological Centre in Boston. She is currently writing a PhD dissertation in Systematic Theology, entitled 'The Voices of

Asian Women in the Contextualisations of Asian Theologies'. Two of her essays are forthcoming: 'Following Naked Dancing and Long Dreaming' in *Inheriting Our Mothers' Gardens: Feminist Theology in Third World Perspective* (1987) and 'Hanpuri: Doing Theology from a Korean Women's Perspective' in *Ecumenical Review* (1988).

JAMES CONE received his BA from Philander Smith College in Little Rock, Arkansas, his BD from Garrett Theological Seminary, and his MA and PhD from Garrett Theological Seminary, and his MA and PhD from Northwestern University in Evanston, Illinois. His publications include: *Black Theology and Black Power* (1969); *A Black Theology of Liberation* (1970); *The Spirituals and the Blues: An Interpretation* (1972); *God of the Oppressed* (1975); *Black Theology: A Documentary History 1966–1979*, edited with Gayraud S. Wilmore (1979); *My Soul Looks Back* (1987); *For My People* (1984); *Speaking the Truth* (1986). At present he is Briggs Distinguished Professor of Systematic Theology at Union Theological Seminary in New York.

DOROTHY FOLLIARD is a Dominican sister of the Adrian, Michigan Congregation. She holds a PhD in Latin and Greek (University of Michigan) and degrees in theology and scripture from the University of Chicago Divinity School and Loyola University, Chicago. She is an experienced educator in secondary and college levels. Dorothy Folliard was a contributor to position paper, 'The Ordination of Women', sponsored by the US Dominican Leadership Conference 1978. She is currently teaching in the pastoral institute of the Mexican American Cultural Centre, San Antonio, Texas.

SERGIO TORRES GONZALEZ was born at Talca, Chile, in 1929. He is a Catholic priest and a graduate in theology of the Catholic University of Chile. He continued his studies at the Gregorian University in Rome and at the Brussels Centre for Socio-Religious Research. He has spent most of his time in pastoral co-ordination work in Talca diocese, Chile. He has been pastoral secretary and vicar general to Bishops Manuel Larrain and Carlos Gonzalez. He spent some years in New York, working with Spanish speakers in Spanish parishes. Simultaneously he took part in the 'Theology in the Americas' project was a founder-member of the 'Ecumenical Association of Third World Theologians'. He is now parish priest at San Lucas in Santiago and professor of systematic theology at the Alphonsine Institute of Theology and Pastoral Studies. Among his publications are *La Reforma*

Agraria en America Latina (Madrid 1962) and editions of various papers given at conferences of the Ecumenical Association of Third World Theologians: for example, *The Emergent Gospel; The Challenge of Basic Christian Communities; Doing Theology in a Divided World.* All his books were first published in English and have been translated into various languages.

PROFESSOR ENGELBERT MVENG SJ was born in 1930. A Jesuit since 1951, he was ordained Priest in 1963. He studied at the Universities of Dakar (Senegal), Namur and Louvain (Belgium) and took his doctorate at the University of Paris (Sorbonne). Since 1965 he has taught at the University of Yaoundé (Cameroon), and is currently Secretary General of the Ecumenical Association of African Theologians. His publications number about twenty titles on History, Art, Anthropology, Spirituality, Poetry and Theology.

TISSA BALASURIYA OMI is the author of *Jesus Christ and Human Liberation* (1976); *Eucharist and Human Liberation* (1977); *Planetary Theology* (1984); *Sri Lanka Economy in Crisis* (1981); *Catastrophe July 1873* and many pamphlets and articles.

SAMUEL RAYAN was born 1920 and entered the Society of Jesus 1939. He was ordained priest 1955 and gained a doctorate in theology 1960 at the Gregorian University in Rome. He was Chaplain to University Students Organization in Kerala from 1961 until 1972 and has been Professor of theology, Vidya Jyoti, Delhi, since then. He served as member on WCC Commission on Faith and Order, 1968–1982. He is sectional editor of *Jeevadhara*, journal of theology. His publications include *The Holy Spirit* (New York 1978); *The Anger of God* (Bombay 1982); *In Christ: The Power of Women* (Madras 1986).

PABLO RICHARD was born in 1939 in Chile. He was educated in Chile (1966) and at the Pontifical Biblical Institute in Rome (1969). He has a doctorate in the sociology of religion from the Sorbonne (1978) and a doctorate *honoris causa* from the Free Faculty of Protestant Theology in Paris. At present, he is professor of theology at the National University and a member of the Ecumenical Research Despartment in Costa Rica; this department prepares pastoral agents for the Basic Ecclesial Communities in Central America. His latest books include *La Iglesia latinoamericana entre el temor y la esperanza* (San José 1987) 4th. edition, which has been translated into Portuguese, Italian and French; *Morte das cristiandades e nascimento da Igreja* (São Paulo 1984), 2nd. edition, which has been translated into French and English—English title, *Death of Christendoms, Birth of the Church* (Orbis 1988); and *La fuerza espiritual de la Iglesia de los pobres* with a preface by Leonardo Boff (San José 1987).

JULIO DE SANTA ANA was born in Montevideo, Uruguay in 1934. He belongs to the Methodist Church. He studied theology in Buenos Aires and obtained a doctorate in Religious Sciences from the University of Strasbourg. He was director of the River Plate Centre for Christian Studies; Secretary General of the Church and Society in Latin America movement (ISAL); Director of the Department of Cultural Extension of the University of Montevideo; Secretary of Studies and later Director of the World Council of Churches' Commission for Church Participation in Development. At present he is co-Director of the Ecumenical Centre of Services for Evangelisation and Popular Education (CESEP) and Co-ordinator of the Centre for Post-graduate Studies in Religious Sciences at the Methodist Institute of Higher Studies in São Paulo, Brazil. His many articles and books include *Good News to the Poor*; *Pan, Vino y Amistad*; *Ecumenismo y Liberación*.

JUSTIN UKPONG is dean of the theological faculty of the Catholic Institute of West Africa, Port Harcourt, Nigeria, where he teaches New Testament and African theology. He is also editor of *Incarnation*, the Institute's academic journal. Publications include *African Theologies Now: A Profile* (1984); *Sacrifice: African and Biblical* (1987); *African Theology: An Introduction* (1988). He is current preparing a book on Mission in Acts of the Apostles from a Third World Perspective.

CONCILIUM

88. **Polarization in the Church.** Ed. Hans Küng and Walter Kasper. 0 8164 2572 8 156pp.

89. **Spiritual Revivals.** Ed. Christian Duquoc and Casiano Floristán. 0 8164 2573 6 156pp.

90. **Power and the Word of God.** Ed. Franz Bockle and Jacques Marie Pohier. 0 8164 2574 4 156pp.

91. **The Church as Institution.** Ed. Gregory Baum and Andrew Greeley. 0 8164 2575 2 168pp.

92. **Politics and Liturgy.** Ed. Herman Schmidt and David Power. 0 8164 2576 0 156pp.

93. **Jesus Christ and Human Freedom.** Ed. Edward Schillebeeckx and Bas van Iersel. 0 8164 2577 9 168pp.

94. **The Experience of Dying.** Ed. Norbert Greinacher and Alois Müller. 0 8164 2578 7 156pp.

95. **Theology of Joy.** Ed. Johannes Baptist Metz and Jean-Pierre Jossua. 0 8164 2579 5 164pp.

96. **The Mystical and Political Dimension of the Christian Faith.** Ed. Claude Geffré and Gustavo Guttierez. 0 8164 2580 9 168pp.

97. **The Future of the Religious Life.** Ed. Peter Huizing and William Bassett. 0 8164 2094 7 96pp.

98. **Christians and Jews.** Ed. Hans Küng and Walter Kasper. 0 8164 2095 5 96pp.

99. **Experience of the Spirit.** Ed. Peter Huizing and William Bassett. 0 8164 2096 3 144pp.

100. **Sexuality in Contemporary Catholicism.** Ed. Franz Bockle and Jacques Marie Pohier. 0 8164 2097 1 126pp.

101. **Ethnicity.** Ed. Andrew Greeley and Gregory Baum. 0 8164 2145 5 120pp.

102. **Liturgy and Cultural Religious Traditions.** Ed. Herman Schmidt and David Power. 0 8164 2146 2 120pp.

103. **A Personal God?** Ed. Edward Schillebeeckx and Bas van Iersel. 0 8164 2149 8 142pp.

104. **The Poor and the Church.** Ed. Norbert Greinacher and Alois Müller. 0 8164 2147 1 128pp.

105. **Christianity and Socialism.** Ed. Johannes Baptist Metz and Jean-Pierre Jossua. 0 8164 2148 X 144pp.

106. **The Churches of Africa: Future Prospects.** Ed. Claude Geffré and Bertrand Luneau. 0 8164 2150 1 128pp.

107. **Judgement in the Church.** Ed. William Bassett and Peter Huizing. 0 8164 2166 8 128pp.

108. **Why Did God Make Me?** Ed. Hans Küng and Jürgen Moltmann. 0 8164 2167 6 112pp.

109. **Charisms in the Church.** Ed. Christian Duquoc and Casiano Floristán. 0 8164 2168 4 128pp.

110. **Moral Formation and Christianity.** Ed. Franz Bockle and Jacques Marie Pohier. 0 8164 2169 2 120pp.

111. **Communication in the Church.** Ed. Gregory Baum and Andrew Greeley. 0 8164 2170 6 126pp.

112. **Liturgy and Human Passage.** Ed. David Power and Luis Maldonado. 0 8164 2608 2 136pp.

113. **Revelation and Experience.** Ed. Edward Schillebeeckx and Bas van Iersel. 0 8164 2609 0 134pp.

114. **Evangelization in the World Today.** Ed. Norbert Greinacher and Alois Müller. 0 8164 2610 4 136pp.

115. **Doing Theology in New Places.** Ed. Jean-Pierre Jossua and Johannes Baptist Metz. 0 8164 2611 2 120pp.

116. **Buddhism and Christianity.** Ed. Claude Geffré and Mariasusai Dhavamony. 0 8164 2612 0 136pp.

117. **The Finances of the Church.** Ed. William Bassett and Peter Huizing. 0 8164 2197 8 160pp.

118. **An Ecumenical Confession of Faith?** Ed. Hans Küng and Jürgen Moltmann. 0 8164 2198 6 136pp.

119. **Discernment of the Spirit and of Spirits.** Ed. Casiano Floristán and Christian Duquoc. 0 8164 2199 4 136pp.

120. **The Death Penalty and Torture.** Ed. Franz Bockle and Jacques Marie Pohier. 0 8164 2200 1 136pp.

121. **The Family in Crisis or in Transition.** Ed. Andrew Greeley. 0 567 30001 3 128pp.

122. **Structures of Initiation in Crisis.** Ed. Luis Maldonado and David Power. 0 567 30002 1 128pp.

123. **Heaven.** Ed. Bas van Iersel and Edward Schillebeeckx. 0 567 30003 X 120pp.

124. **The Church and the Rights of Man.** Ed. Alois Müller and Norbert Greinacher. 0 567 30004 8 140pp.

125. **Christianity and the Bourgeoisie.** Ed. Johannes Baptist Metz. 0 567 30005 6 144pp.

126. **China as a Challenge to the Church.** Ed. Claude Geffré and Joseph Spae. 0 567 30006 4 136pp.

127. **The Roman Curia and the Communion of Churches.** Ed. Peter Huizing and Knut Walf. 0 567 30007 2 144pp.

128. **Conflicts about the Holy Spirit.** Ed. Hans Küng and Jürgen Moltmann. 0 567 30008 0 144pp.

129. **Models of Holiness.** Ed. Christian Duquoc and Casiano Floristán. 0 567 30009 9 128pp.

130. **The Dignity of the Despised of the Earth.** Ed. Jacques Marie Pohier and Dietmar Mieth. 0 567 30010 2 144pp.

131. **Work and Religion.** Ed. Gregory Baum. 0 567 30011 0 148pp.

132. **Symbol and Art in Worship.** Ed. Luis Maldonado and David Power. 0 567 30012 9 136pp.

133. **Right of the Community to a Priest.** Ed. Edward Schillebeeckx and Johannes Baptist Metz. 0 567 30013 7 148pp.

134. **Women in a Men's Church.** Ed. Virgil Elizondo and Norbert Greinacher. 0 567 30014 5 144pp.

135. **True and False Universality of Christianity.** Ed. Claude Geffré and Jean-Pierre Jossua. 0 567 30015 3 138pp.

136. **What is Religion? An Inquiry for Christian Theology.** Ed. Mircea Eliade and David Tracy. 0 567 30016 1 98pp.

137. **Electing our Own Bishops.** Ed. Peter Huizing and Knut Walf. 0 567 30017 X 112pp.

138. **Conflicting Ways of Interpreting the Bible.** Ed. Hans Küng and Jürgen Moltmann. 0 567 30018 8 112pp.

139. **Christian Obedience.** Ed. Casiano Floristán and Christian Duquoc. 0 567 30019 6 96pp.

140. **Christian Ethics and Economics: the North-South Conflict.** Ed. Dietmar Mieth and Jacques Marie Pohier. 0 567 30020 X 128pp.

141. **Neo-Conservatism: Social and Religious Phenomenon.** Ed. Gregory Baum and John Coleman. 0 567 30021 8.

142. **The Times of Celebration.** Ed. David Power and Mary Collins. 0 567 30022 6.

143. **God as Father.** Ed. Edward Schillebeeckx and Johannes Baptist Metz. 0 567 30023 4.

144. **Tensions Between the Churches of the First World and the Third World.** Ed. Virgil Elizondo and Norbert Greinacher. 0 567 30024 2.

145. **Nietzsche and Christianity.** Ed. Claude Geffré and Jean-Pierre Jossua. 0 567 30025 0.

146. **Where Does the Church Stand?** Ed. Giuseppe Alberigo. 0 567 30026 9.

147. **The Revised Code of Canon Law: a Missed Opportunity?** Ed. Peter Huizing and Knut Walf. 0 567 30027 7.

148. **Who Has the Say in the Church?** Ed. Hans Küng and Jürgen Moltmann. 0 567 30028 5.

149. **Francis of Assisi Today.** Ed. Casiano Floristán and Christian Duquoc. 0 567 30029 3.

150. **Christian Ethics: Uniformity, Universality, Pluralism.** Ed. Jacques Pohier and Dietmar Mieth. 0 567 30030 7.

151. **The Church and Racism.** Ed. Gregory Baum and John Coleman. 0 567 30031 5.

152. **Can we always celebrate the Eucharist?** Ed. Mary Collins and David Power. 0 567 30032 3.

153. **Jesus, Son of God?** Ed. Edward Schillebeeckx and Johannes-Baptist Metz. 0 567 30033 1.

154. **Religion and Churches in Eastern Europe.** Ed. Virgil ELizondo and Norbert Greinacher. 0 567 30034 X.

155. **'The Human', Criterion of Christian Existence?** Ed. Claude Geffré and Jean-Pierre Jossua. 0 567 30035 8.

156. **The Challenge of Psychology to Faith.** Ed. Steven Kepnes (Guest Editor) and David Tracy. 0 567 30036 6.

157. **May Church Ministers be Politicians?** Ed. Peter Huizing and Knut Walf. 0 567 30037 4.

158. **The Right to Dissent.** Ed. Hans Küng and Jürgen Moltmann. 0 567 30038 2.

CONCILIUM

CONCILIUM 1987

All back issues are still in print: available from bookshops (price £5.45) or direct from the publishers (£5.95/US$9.95/Can$11.75 including postage and packing).

T & T CLARK LTD, 59 GEORGE STREET EDINBURGH EH2 2LQ, SCOTLAND

Pillars of Flame
Power, Priesthood and Spiritual Maturity
Maggie Ross

'My vocation is to Christ's priesthood in my being, not to function as part of the ordained secular power that currently organizes the church.' Critical of church structures, Maggie Ross outlines a spirituality with a positive evaluation of the non-ordained of the church.

£8.50   *paper*

Ethics and Liberation
An Introduction
Charles L Kammer

Provides guidelines for responsible stands on contemporary issues, be they personal or socio-political, and a clear introduction to the basic question, 'How does one *do* Christian ethics in a pluralistic world?'

£10.50   *paper*

Theology from the Womb of Asia
Choan-Seng Song

Faith explored in the midst of Asian culture to establish an indigenous theology

£8.95   *paper*

The Dialogical Imperative
A Christian Reflection on Interfaith Encounter
David Lochhead

Shows why faithfulness to Jesus Christ makes inter-religious dialogue a Christian imperative.

£5.50   *paper*

SCM Press Ltd
26–30 Tottenham Road, London N1 4BZ

0